Praise for *The Happiest Life*

"We become what we do, and Hugh Hewitt's career testifies to his good will, his faith, the love he bears for his family, his generous humor, and his erudition on an astonishing range of history, politics, current events, and literature. No one commands a topic or marshals an argument as skillfully as Hugh; yet he does both with unfailing courtesy. That spirit is alive on every page of this book. *The Happiest Life* is not simply a delight to read, and not merely a glimpse under the hood of a remarkable man. It's a map to what Robert Frost once described as the road less traveled—the road that leads to a life of meaning and gratitude and joy."

—CHARLES J. CHAPUT, O.F.M. CAP.,
ARCHBISHOP OF PHILADELPHIA

"To put it straight, Hugh Hewitt is one of the most intelligent and enthusiastic people I know. In his new book, *The Happiest Life*, both of these qualities come out: wise advice and an enthusiasm for life. Reading this book is the next best thing to sitting down for a long conversation with my friend Hugh Hewitt."

—DR. R. ALBERT MOHLER, JR.,
PRESIDENT OF THE SOUTHERN
BAPTIST THEOLOGICAL SEMINARY

"Wanna be a happier person? Know anyone else who does? What if this book could actually help with that? Cutting to the chase—*it can*. And it will. It will change lives. I cannot think of a book more fit to give away indiscriminately to anyone I know. The winsome wisdom within its eminently readable pages is worth more than gold. Where has this book been all our lives? Am I gushing? Good."

—ERIC METAXAS, *NEW YORK TIMES* BEST-
SELLING AUTHOR OF *BONHOEFFER: PASTOR,
MARTYR, PROPHET, SPY* AND *7 MEN: AND
THE SECRET OF THEIR GREATNESS*

"In these polarized times, it's a blessing to find someone like Hugh Hewitt who reaches across the chasm of ugliness with such wisdom and good cheer. He's a happy warrior and this book is a road map for helping make the rest of us—liberals and conservatives alike (yes, alike)—happier, too."

—JONATHAN ALTER, AUTHOR OF *THE CENTER HOLDS: OBAMA AND HIS ENEMIES*

"Hugh's *The Happiest Life* is a powerful look at what can increase happiness. I enjoyed reading his insights on traits like empathy and gratitude that benefit both their object and their source. I especially appreciated Hugh sharing his personal experiences, such as his visit with President George W. Bush. I would highly recommend *The Happiest Life* and commend Hugh for writing such a heartfelt and thoughtful work that will help any reader understand the moral life."

—KARL ROVE, FORMER DEPUTY CHIEF OF STAFF AND SENIOR ADVISOR TO PRESIDENT GEORGE W. BUSH; AUTHOR OF *COURAGE AND CONSEQUENCE*

"Hugh Hewitt brings gifts to his country, to his radio listeners, and to his law students who are precious. He is intelligent, enthusiastic for the best things and he never tires of pursuing them. Of course, his friends get this gift best of all, and I have been proud to be among them. Read this book. It is just like Hugh."

—DR. ARNN, PRESIDENT, HILLSDALE COLLEGE

"Hugh Hewitt's *The Happiest Life* is a must read for anyone looking for the practical way to help themselves and improve the lives of others. Through the lens of his own life experiences, Hewitt reveals in this beautifully written book the paradoxical truth that freely giving away what we value most is what makes us fully alive. Beyond simply advocating conventional money donations, *The Happiest Life* will convince readers to get serious about giving away their precious time, talent, attention, and affection—and thus reveal their own best selves."

—ARTHUR C. BROOKS, PRESIDENT OF THE AMERICAN ENTERPRISE INSTITUTE AND AUTHOR OF *THE ROAD TO FREEDOM*

"Hugh Hewitt has written a riveting memoir, a beautiful spiritual confession, a glorious ode to life, and a moving expression of gratitude for the unique life this good man has lived and continues to live. One puts the book down wishing it were longer—but unquestionably happier for having read it. What more can anyone ask from any book?"

—DENNIS PRAGER, NATIONALLY
SYNDICATED TALK SHOW HOST, *NEW
YORK TIMES* BEST-SELLING AUTHOR, AND
FOUNDER OF PRAGERUNIVERSITY.COM

"Hugh Hewitt is a happy man and he is also the cause of happiness in others. He has discovered the secret of happiness. It is a secret sought by many and discovered through deep thought or natural inclination only by a few. I have seen Hugh act on his understanding of happiness many times since I first met him and been struck by the fact that I have never met anyone quite like him. Indeed, I stand in awe of him. Now I understand why. In this book Hugh happily shares the secret of happiness with his readers. This is therefore a book that gives the gift that keeps on giving. I am most grateful for it. It belongs on the bookshelf along with classic reflections on the sources of happiness by Aristotle and Thomas Aquinas and C. S. Lewis."

—SCOTT W. JOHNSON, *POWERLINE*

"Hugh Hewitt's expansive, enthusiastic, and buoyant spirit is the animating force behind *The Happiest Life*, his most personal, most timeless, and most necessary book."

—JOHN PODHORETZ,
EDITOR OF *COMMENTARY*

"Hugh Hewitt is many things, but I think of him as one of the nation's teachers. Here he teaches us how to flourish as human beings—one of the oldest lessons taught by public intellectuals from Greece to now. Hewitt is a man in the arena, intellectual and political, and in a better time would be a Solon, but we can benefit from his wisdom as one of our leaders of the political and cultural opposition."

—JOHN MARK REYNOLDS, PROVOST
AND PROFESSOR OF PHILOSOPHY AT
HOUSTON BAPTIST UNIVERSITY

"Hugh Hewitt talks about the gifts we can give each other to make life better . . . I say, start with this book. It can make an impact in every life, helping us to be content even in the most demanding circumstances. This may be Hugh Hewitt's most important book!"

—TERRY PLUTO,
CLEVELAND PLAIN DEALER

"This is a delightfully cheerful book—chock-full of mature, insightful wisdom about some 'secrets' of a happy life that are sadly forgotten today. I expect that people who read it will find themselves, as I did, both personally challenged and also wanting to give a copy to everyone they know."

—WAYNE GRUDEM, PH.D.,
RESEARCH PROFESSOR OF THEOLOGY
AND BIBLICAL STUDIES, PHOENIX
SEMINARY, PHOENIX, ARIZONA

"In this thoughtful new book, Hugh Hewitt claims to offer the 'secrets to being, for the most part, happy.' He delivers, offering a remarkable treatise that identifies generosity as the key to human happiness. *The Happiest Life* is one of those wonderful books that make you feel like somebody has finally put into words those essential truths that we all feel, deep down in our souls."

—JAY COST, *THE WEEKLY STANDARD*

"*The Happiest Life* is a marvelous book—engaging, wise, and eminently readable. It's filled with stories about fascinating people and teaches us, in a winsome and winning way, important moral truths. Hugh Hewitt's enthusiasm for life—and his devotion to his faith—radiates throughout the book. Read *The Happiest Life*. Reflect on it. You'll be better for it. And happier, too."

—PETE WEHNER, SENIOR FELLOW AT
THE ETHICS AND PUBLIC POLICY CENTER

THE
HAPPIEST
LIFE

THE

HAPPIEST LIFE

SEVEN GIFTS, SEVEN GIVERS & THE
SECRET TO GENUINE SUCCESS

HUGH HEWITT

NELSON
BOOKS
An Imprint of Thomas Nelson

Published in Nashville, Tennessee, by Nelson Books, an imprint of Thomas Nelson. Nelson Books and Thomas Nelson are registered trademarks of HarperCollins Christian Publishing, Inc.

Thomas Nelson, Inc., titles may be purchased in bulk for educational, business, fund-raising, or sales promotional use. For information, please e-mail SpecialMarkets@ThomasNelson.com.

Unless otherwise noted, Scripture quotations are taken from THE NEW KING JAMES VERSION. © 1982 by Thomas Nelson, Inc. Used by permission. All rights reserved.

Scripture quotations marked NIV are taken from the Holy Bible, New International Version®, NIV®. Copyright © 1973, 1978, 1984 by Biblica, Inc.™ Used by permission of Zondervan. All rights reserved worldwide. www.zondervan.com.

Scripture quotations marked RSV are from THE ENGLISH STANDARD VERSION. © 2001 by Crossway Bibles, a division of Good News Publishers. REVISED STANDARD VERSION of the Bible. © 1946, 1952, 1971, 1973 by the Division of Christian Education of the National Council of the Churches of Christ in the U.S.A. Used by permission.

ISBN: 978-0-52910-272-0 (IE)

Library of Congress Cataloging-in-Publication Data

Hewitt, Hugh, 1956-
 The happiest life : seven gifts, seven givers, and the secret to genuine success / Hugh Hewitt.
  pages cm
 Includes bibliographical references.
 ISBN 978-1-59555-578-6
1. Generosity—Religious aspects—Christianity. 2. Happiness—Religious aspects—Christianity. I. Title.
 BV4647.G45H49 2013
 248.4—dc23

2013027017

Printed in the United States of America

13 14 15 16 17 RRD 6 5 4 3 2 1

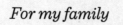

For my family

Finally, brethren, whatever things are true, whatever things are noble, whatever things are just, whatever things are pure, whatever things are lovely, whatever things are of good report, if there is any virtue and if there is anything praiseworthy—meditate on these things.

—THE EPISTLE TO THE PHILIPPIANS

CONTENTS

Introduction: Gifts and Givers　　　xiii

The Precondition of Generosity　　　xxi

Part One: The Seven Gifts

The First Gift: Encouragement　　　3

The Second Gift: Energy　　　11

The Third Gift: Enthusiasm　　　19

The Fourth Gift: Empathy　　　29

The Fifth Gift: Good Humor　　　39

The Sixth Gift: Graciousness　　　49

The Seventh Gift: Gratitude　　　57

Part Two: The Seven Givers

The First Giver: The Spouse　　　73

The Second Giver: The Parent　　　81

The Third Giver: Family Members　　　91

The Fourth Giver: Friends　　　97

The Fifth Giver: The Coworker　　　105

The Sixth Giver: Teachers　　　119

CONTENTS

The Seventh Giver: The Church   133

The Greatest Giver   149

Conclusion   157

Acknowledgments   167

Index   169

About the Author   177

INTRODUCTION
GIFTS AND GIVERS

*The secret to happiness is freedom, and the secret to
freedom is courage.*

—THUCYDIDES

COURAGE UNDERGIRDS EVERY GOOD THING. COURAGE IS,
as has long been said, the first virtue because it allows all other
virtues to flourish. It takes courage to look clearly forward and
backward, and to make a change in direction that increases happiness and human flourishing. This is a book about the courage
to give and receive the best gifts that this wonderful life can offer
to both giver and receiver.

It takes a little courage even to talk about this gift giving
with your spouse and family, and a lot of courage to change your
ways when it comes to being a taker in order to become a giver.
Perhaps this book will help.

I am writing it to prod my children to remember that these
are the things that motivated their parents and which we hope
will continue to motivate them. If other parents give other

children the book to help them reach the same conclusions, it will have succeeded beyond my greatest hopes.

Almost every parent I have known agrees with the statement that a mother or a father is only as happy as their least happy child. Most agree that they are happiest when their children are giving and receiving gifts among themselves—genuine gifts of whatever value, or of no monetary value at all. Giving and receiving among children is a wondrous thing for a parent to behold.

The observations on happiness that follow are not unique or new. They've been bouncing around the world for centuries. Aristotle's *Nicomachean Ethics*, written more than twenty-three hundred years ago, is concerned primarily with achieving happiness, the "Chief Good," as he put it.

I have no claim of expertise on the conditions that produce human happiness, other than having been, for the most part, very happy throughout my life. I have, however, made a career for the past twenty-four years of interviewing people for radio and television. That allowed me to observe a lot of very different people at pretty close range and to read a great number of very different books. I figured out that I have now interviewed far more than ten thousand people, perhaps even double that number. That doesn't include callers to my radio show. A lot of the people I interviewed had written books, which I read before the author appeared. Unlike most talk show hosts, I have managed to read the books of nine out of ten authors who have appeared on the show.

The list of those interviews, authors and nonauthors alike, is pretty remarkable, and includes the very powerful, the very famous, the very rich, and the very good. For just one example, I interviewed His Holiness the Dalai Lama for three hours. So, to quote the estimable Bill Murray in *Caddyshack*, "I've got that going for me."

But whether it is President George W. Bush or Julie Andrews, Michael Dell or Justice Stephen Breyer, or any of the other thousands of interviewees, they all began life helpless and will all end it dead; and in between they will have hoped to be happy for at least some of the time. As my friend Dennis Prager says, "Happiness is a serious problem." He is right, of course. Happiness, real and genuine happiness, is the essence of a life well lived.

Only recently in my broadcast career did I begin to wrestle with happiness on air, in early 2013. I did so with the assistance of Dr. Larry Arnn, the president of Hillsdale College, who has for many, many years been my teacher.

I had begun to consider writing about happiness the previous summer when my friend Dr. Jack Templeton gave me his little book *Thrift and Generosity: The Joy of Giving*, which I heartily recommend to you. Jack and his wonderful wife, Dr. Pina Templeton, have spent a lifetime helping others, and his compact book condenses all that experience as well as the wisdom of his father, Sir John Templeton, into an easy-to-absorb primer on happiness.

Aristotle, on the other hand, is not so easy to absorb. Very difficult, in fact. Which is why I turned to Larry Arnn for help.

Over the years Larry has often joined me on air for long talks about big subjects. Almost a decade ago he allowed me to march him through a "history of ideas" that spanned two broadcast days—six radio hours—that so charmed the audience that it has played the last broadcast day of every December and the first broadcast day of every January since it was first recorded.

Larry Arnn, like most of the faculty at Hillsdale College, is a remarkable teacher, so, believing radio to be uniquely positioned to deliver content about big ideas in a coherent, useful way, I asked him if he and his colleagues would undertake a "Great Books on the Radio" series at the beginning of 2013, to which he agreed. The last hour of every Friday's broadcast is now given over to a conversation with Dr. Arnn or one of his distinguished colleagues—Dr. Paul Rahe, Dr. Thomas West, or others—on one of the greatest works of the West, such as *The Illiad*, the Hebrew and Christian Scriptures (this took many weeks), Herodotus, Thucydides, various works of Plato, and on through the canon.

These conversations were instantly beloved by some, hated by others, and a source of controversy among a few radio professionals who wondered whether a general radio audience would (or could) actually listen to a broadcast hour on such topics.

That debate is now over, as the audience became larger and larger and more and more enthusiastic. Here were conversations worth having and hearing. And the most important of those conversations? The four hours devoted to Aristotle's *Nicomachean Ethics*, the book about achieving happiness.

My life is now fifty-eight years along, an age by which my two grandmothers had both waved good-bye to this world. Fifty-eight was barely the third quarter for my Gramps, A. T. Rohl, who made it on his own wheels and in his own house to the age of 101. My other grandfather, for whom I was named and to whom I owe a few thousand chuckles from long-distance operators and call-center handlers, made it to ninety-one. Whether I have inherited my grandmothers' brevity genes or A. T.'s and Grandfather Hugh's long-distance DNA remains to be seen; but in either case, it is time to write down my observations on the secrets to being, for the most part, happy.

Let me hasten to explain that "for the most part." As you might have guessed, it is a key qualifier, a very important one. Nobody gets out of here without pain or sorrow along the way. "Nobody has the perfect package," said my pal Coach Jerry again and again, who like all coaches was a font of condensed wisdom, repeated often. This hard reality about the inevitability of hardship and grief is crucial to the happiness that the seven gifts make possible. Which gifts? I'm coming to those.

As I noted above, I began this book with my three children in mind, with the hope that it would contribute to their happiness and their children's. It is about the seven genuine gifts that they can give and receive from each other and from others—especially their own spouses and children—and why I believe the act of giving those gifts produces happiness.

They will laugh at the first thought of their dad as a gift giver, as I am a notoriously bad selector of presents—famously so within my family and among my friends. The Fetching Mrs. Hewitt, as I call my wonderful wife when I'm on the radio, has been on the receiving end of at least one thousand presents over the thirty-plus years of our marriage, and I am being overly generous with myself when I say that more than 90 percent have been returned as "swing-and-a-miss" gifts. This is why Nordstrom is so crucial to my marriage. "No harm, no foul" is the rule at Nordstrom with its famous no-questions-asked return policy, and over the years Betsy has shared a few chuckles with the sales associates at Nordstrom on the woeful taste of her husband in pretty much everything to do with women's gifts.

My daughter has similar stories about my lack of present-giving acuity, which she believes must be intentional because my gift giving is so often off the mark. My boys, of course, had some years of good loot when soldiers, action figures, play weapons, and gift cards appeared under the tree. I am a pretty good bet for the early years of any grandchild as well, since big, brightly colored blocks, Playmobil figures, LEGOS, and Tub People books are easy to come by.

But generally I stick to cash, and my colleagues who help me run the show and my law firm are the happier for my giving of checks and not cheesecakes.

Thankfully, my lack of skill at selecting presents doesn't figure in this book. Presents are not the gifts I am writing about here. These gifts, of which I have tried to be a profligate giver, are far more consequential than shoes and purses, iPads and basketball tickets.

These are the gifts that in turn produce happiness in their recipient, and therefore in the giver. They are:

1. Encouragement
2. Energy
3. Enthusiasm
4. Empathy
5. Good Humor
6. Graciousness
7. Gratitude

Everyone is eligible to be a giver of these gifts. Everyone. You don't need wealth. You don't have to be twenty-one. You don't even have to be literate.

That said, some people are particularly well placed to give some of these gifts at particular times. I deal with this in part 2, which covers the seven different givers of these gifts: spouses, parents, family members, friends, coworkers, teachers, and members of a church congregation. Those roles are theoretically open to all readers at some point in their lives.

The one job not open to anyone—that of God—does, however, present a relationship available to everyone and is ultimately the source of all good gifts and the impulse to give them; and so I conclude the book with a reflection on God as the first giver of the greatest gifts. Throughout these chapters are the stories I have lived that allow me to illustrate each of these gifts.

Each of these unique gifts can actually be bestowed on other people. They can be, in a word, transferred. Thus they are "gifts."

Each of these unique gifts bestows a particular grace on the recipient and endows the giver with a particular grace as well.

Each can be given repeatedly; and with the practice of giving, expertise will grow in that particular practice.

Some people practice their golf games. Others practice their patience. The latter will be happier. By far. So it is with all the gifts.

In addition to the seven gifts and the seven givers, there is also a singular characteristic, a behavior, that accompanies all the gifts when given in a particular way, one that while not a potential gift that can be actually and specifically given, is a pattern of conduct that can be modeled. In modeling, it can be of enormous influence on everyone in your life. I begin by looking at this behavior—generosity—as it is the key to all the other gifts. It's a multiplier of every gift given by every giver.

Underlying generosity is that virtue I began this chapter by noting: courage. You have to have the courage to give away what you hold dearest, again and again and again. Every day. Remarkably, self-sacrifice and generosity produce the greatest, most enduring happiness.

Some might find parts of this book uncomfortable. Very uncomfortable, in fact. But it is true as far as I know truth. And the first truth is that the most generous people I have known have been the happiest.

THE PRECONDITION OF GENEROSITY

He who sows bountifully will also reap bountifully.

—The Second Letter to the Corinthians

THE MOST GENEROUS MAN I HAD EVER KNOWN WAS dying.

Tom's breathing was labored. He had been on a morphine drip for a few days, and he pressed it midway through our last hour together. He could speak only in snatches, and he dozed throughout. One of his sons, Joey, came in to say he was off to practice and that he loved his dad. His dad replied that he loved his son and, after Joey left, Tom told me of his immense pride in his son's water polo skills and his future at UCLA where he would begin that fall.

Tom's wonderful wife, Jolene—"She did it all," he said of the raising of their children—and his daughter, Michelle, were downstairs watching a movie and chatting as they supported each other through the last days of Tom's long and difficult struggle. Michelle was home from Alabama where she was pursuing a PhD, another source of enormous pride for Tom that he spoke about that night. Tom wasn't an academic, but was pleased and more than a little amazed that he and Jolene had produced a scholar.

I didn't see Tom's other son, Tj, that evening, but Tom and I talked about how happy I had been to cast a vote for Tj a day earlier when I filled out my absentee ballot and checked Tj's name for the GOP Central Committee in California's Orange County. Tom slowly stated his enormous pride in also having been able to vote for his son for a position he himself had held for decades.

Tom Fuentes served as the chairman of Orange County's Republican Party for twenty years, building by far the most effective county party organization in the country. He was a deeply conservative man, a devout Roman Catholic, and an aggressive defender of the Reagan legacy that he had helped build when Reagan was beginning his career as a national politician. He nurtured that career all the way through the Gipper's presidency, the value of which he never doubted.

Tom had traveled the world supporting freedom and faith, one year collecting musical instruments for schoolchildren in Nicaragua, the next driving back and forth with goods for the impoverished in small towns south of the US–Mexico border, the third founding and helping fund a food bank for the least well-off in Orange County. As a Knight of Malta, he had personally made many trips to Lourdes to help the sick into the waters in search of a blessing and a cure.

Tom poured himself into mentoring hundreds of young activists in politics, giving them advice, jobs, contacts, and always encouragement. He was a very good husband to a very good wife, the proud and strong father of three wonderful children, and a great friend to more people than you can imagine.

He was the most generous man I have ever met, and as I left him that night I told him so. When I gave a eulogy for Tom a week later, I began by saying the very same thing. Four other friends, all three of his children, and three priests spoke in the course of a vigil, a funeral, and a graveside service. Every one of them mentioned his remarkable generosity.

Even as he prepared to exit this life—"I am so ready to go to meet my Father," he told me—he was concerned only about family and friends, eager to point out those who had stood by him through his very long illness.

Talking with Tom that night confirmed for me that the only things that matter in life are God, the people we bless, and those who bless us. As Tom was preparing to leave this world for the next, the big story was the Facebook IPO and the thousand new millionaires it would create along with a few billionaires. It was bracing to consider Tom's pain and dying in that context, and I found myself wondering what the last days of Mark Zuckerberg would be like: if he would be remembered as generous or simply genius, and if the latter would be enough for him. Steve Jobs had died not long before, and the same questions had arisen for me.

We are currently in one of the regularly recurring ages of robber barons, but we always forget the lesson that material wealth simply cannot produce happiness or suggest genuine significance, even time-constrained significance. Nobody cares about Jean Paul Getty anymore, or Henry Ford, though the former has an iconic museum built high over the cultural capital of the world in LA, and the latter has an enormous foundation that carries his name and distributes the benefits of his labor to a huge number of (mostly ungrateful) recipients. One hundred years from now, the Gates Foundation and Zuckerberg's foundation and a hundred other foundations will be functioning, and their founders largely forgotten.

A trip to the ruins of Rome drives this home. You get your span of years. That is all. Nobody cares after you are gone, save for those who loved you; and when they are gone, so is the memory of you.

From this earth. But not from the next life.

Many believe there is good evidence that your happiness in the next life will be a function of your happiness in this life. Christians find that evidence in the words of Christ, throughout the Scripture, and in the testimony of the saints and the best theologians. If only as an insurance policy placed on the chance that I am correct—and not just me but many serious Christian theologians, many from other faiths, and, again, the testimony of Jesus—one ought to study the precondition for happiness.

It isn't money. Really, it's not wealth. "The body of research into what makes people happy is relatively new and small," Jack Templeton concluded at the end of his book, "but the preliminary results unequivocally support what religious teachers have been saying all along: that money really *can't* buy happiness."

Poverty is not an obstacle to happiness, though it may veto health and comfort, and wealth is far from a guarantee of happiness. Wealth might guarantee comfort, but never health. Happiness is only tangentially related to wealth.

Money is, however, related to the seven gifts. But before I begin reviewing my knowledge of those gifts, the necessity of generosity as an attitude needs to be underscored.

Tom Fuentes was the most generous man I have ever known because he was always and everywhere seeking to give something to everyone with whom I saw him come into contact. It was his defining characteristic. Many people who knew him knew that he was relentless in his political activities and in his love for life in its manifestations of good food, wine, travel, and conversation. But if they spent any time at all with him, they also knew Tom was continually seeking to be of assistance to everyone.

I had barely known Tom a couple of months when I first became aware of this. After graduating from Harvard in June of 1978, I moved to California to take a job as a research assistant to David Eisenhower, who had begun writing a book on his grandfather's leadership of the European Theatre in World War II.

I did not know a soul on the West Coast. Before my graduation from college, I had never been farther west than the campus of Notre Dame. But I had been given a name—Bill Dohr—by my pals in College Republicans. When I got to San Clemente, I called Bill and began to make some rounds with him to various GOP events.

At one of those events, I was standing off to the side, a very not-California-looking wonk among a crowd of beautiful strangers. Tom approached me and introduced himself, as he often did to complete strangers at political events. "Hello," he said, "I'm Tom Fuentes. Who are you, and what brings you here?"

The simple act of greeting a stranger is an enormous gesture of hospitality, by the way. Hospitality, like generosity, is not a gift in itself but a precondition of every gift giving of consequence. Gifts matter proportionately with the understanding of who gave them. This idea that knowing who a gift comes from matters conflicts with the idea of the virtue of anonymous charity, and I am not saying that anonymous charity isn't good. It is good—for the giver. But for gifts to have their maximum impact on the recipient, the recipient has to know from whom they are coming. Disguising a gift—either its source or the very fact it is a gift in the first place—denies the opportunity for gratitude to be expressed. This is a key point I will explain later.

Importantly, gratitude is central to understanding God. We practice gratitude with our brothers and sisters on this earth so we are better able to do so with God. Gratitude is the only thing we can give Him, and the only thing He wants, the only thing He cannot simply command if our free will is truly free.

When Tom approached me in the late summer of 1978 at a country club in Dana Point, California, I could not have known, nor could he nor could our mutual friend Bill Dohr have known, that we were launching a three-decade series of dinners that would be highlights of my life—long, discursive, winding chats about everything, among three good pals who had common, yet different, interests.

All those dinners were in the future, but that evening they began to unroll. A couple of weeks later, Tom took Bill and me to the most remarkable restaurant I had ever dined in at that point in my life—Ambrosia, in Newport Beach, California—and although I had been exposed to old-school casual Yankee elegance for many years at Harvard, I had no experience with the formality of high Mexican style. Tom's family had been among the first Mexican families in old California, and he loved to entertain with grace and awareness of the occasion.

Thus launched, the friendship deepened and continued to be full of unexpected gifts, one of which I have told many people about for many years. When I moved to California, I was quite broke. I had a used car, and my father had given me a thousand dollars along with the promise of a safety net should I need to slink back home, defeated in my desire to be in a bigger story than a law practice.

David Eisenhower had agreed to pay me $10,000 for a year's work—in advance!—not bad for 1978, but not high on the hog either. Julie Nixon Eisenhower, one of the most wonderful and kind people I have met along the way, had sought out a furnished one-bedroom apartment for me in the heart of San Clemente's "pier bowl"—"Jartown," as that gritty neighborhood in that town on the border of Camp Pendleton was then called. Not being particularly skilled with money or apartment renting, I thought it best to pay the year's rent in advance rather than risk running out and lacking a place to live. Having plunked down $6,000 to an astonished landlord, I set about living off grilled cheeses and beer, conserving my pennies for an occasional trip up the coast to Newport Beach where Tom and Bill lived.

Tom began with little, but worked always, and had made some dough by the time our paths crossed. He knew my budget and was always finding ways to host me or to allow me to host him in inexpensive ways. He knew that mutuality is a key aspect of friendship.

When Christmas approached, there was no way I had the cash to get home to Ohio for a bit of white Christmas and Browns football. How Tom knew this I don't know, but when he gave me a gift box of Wente wine, I opened it to find a round-trip ticket to Cleveland, a remarkable bit of giving on his part. I have always told people that this gesture impressed upon me the character of Tom as a giver, an impression that was never, ever contradicted in thirty-three years.

Generosity may be a learned behavior, or it may be one of the endowments of Nature and Nature's God. Whichever, it cannot be hidden any more than baldness, bad eyesight, or height. It is a characteristic. It is the most important characteristic, in fact, the one that will define and shape the entirety of a life.

Don't give yourself much time to answer these questions, but run through them:

1. Were your mother and father generous?
2. Is your spouse generous?
3. Are your children, extended family, friends, and coworkers generous?

Rank them quickly in order of least generous to most generous, and then ask yourself which of these people you most enjoy. Generosity is magnetic and charismatic. It beckons, and not out of self-interest, but rather admiration and ease of affection.

Now the hard question: Are you generous? And how about this one: Are you thought to be generous by the same people you just ranked, and to what measure?

Whatever your answers, understand that the gifts that matter cannot be given unless the giver is first generous. Generosity is the first step, the precondition, the necessary ingredient to all the other gifts, and for all those who would be givers.

PART ONE

THE SEVEN GIFTS

THE FIRST GIFT

ENCOURAGEMENT

Let us consider how we may spur one another in order to
stir up love and good works . . .

—THE EPISTLE TO THE HEBREWS

YOU HAVE AN UNLIMITED SUPPLY OF ENCOURAGEMENT
to give. For as long as you draw breath, you can encourage the
people in your life. You don't have to know them, or you may see
or meet them only once. But you can encourage them.

I have a pal, Jan Janura, who is a remarkable man. Jan and
his wife, Carol, began a fashion company many years ago that
many of my women readers will know: Carol Anderson. After
they sold that company, Carol and Jan began CAbi, the largest in-
home clothing line in the world. Jan calls himself a dressmaker,
and credits Carol with all the fashion genius and himself with

3

the smarts to marry her. Together they are extraordinary forces for the good in a thousand ways that I can only assert here for lack of time and space.

Jan's real calling is that of an encourager. Hardly a month goes by when I don't get a card from Jan bearing the quote of some saint or leader exhorting me to aim higher, strive harder, think longer, or pray more fervently. He is always ready with a quick "That was great what you did there," or "Wow, only you could have done that." He reaches into hundreds of lives and says, "More of that, please."

A few years back, Jan read the runaway best seller *Wild at Heart* and was moved by the message of this now-classic work of Christian living for men. Lots of people are. Millions in fact. But Jan did more than admire and resolve to do better in his own life by God and Carol: he resolved to give the gift of *Wild at Heart* to as many men as he could.

First Jan sent dozens and then hundreds of copies to everyone he knew and some people he didn't. He worried, though, that even those who read the book wouldn't "get it," so he began to organize fishing trips to his cabin on the Madison River in Montana—five days of fishing, good food, wine and cigars, and deep conversation about the most serious subjects. One trip became five, and five became ten, and now after years of this calling, more than five hundred men have been on one of these adventures, and that number climbs every year.* In all this he partnered with Ken Tada who smiled, nodded, and executed a vision, complementing Jan's generosity with his own.

I got to know Jan in a roundabout way after hearing about

---

*You can see the full story at jkwa.net and even sign up for an adventure of your own.

him for years. He had begun his post-college life as a staff member for Young Life, one of the great Christian organizations in the world. For eighty years Young Life has reached out to high school students to tell them about Jesus Christ in a way that doesn't send them for the exits before the conversation has begun. This is called "relational ministry" by the deep thinkers, and it has its origin in the accounts we have of Christ's life in the Gospels. Jan was very, very good at being a Young Life leader, but after a few years of being that, he hungered for a life in business and went in search of it.

You never really leave Young Life, as I have learned, and all Jan's Young Life pals remained his pals. One of them is "Bud the Contractor," whom I frequently mention on my radio show and who is my very close friend. Bud is a giver of many, many gifts to me and to many others. Somehow, he got Jan and Carol to start listening to my radio show, which figured in the launch of my friendship with Jan.

My closest friend of many close friends is Bill Lobdell, a former *Los Angeles Times* reporter. Before leaving the news business a few years back, he was the *Times*'s religion reporter and columnist.

Bill picked up this beat after having a profound religious experience at a men's retreat I took him to in the early nineties. Almost everyone who knows anything about Christianity would recognize this as a "born again" moment. Bill was transformed. So he sought and gained the reporting beat that would allow him to tell stories of God at work in the world.

Knowing that, you might be surprised to learn that Bill is also the author of a book titled *Losing My Religion*. It recounts the process by which Bill's faith disappeared. Short version: The

Times assigned him to cover the sexual scandals racking the Roman Catholic Church. Bill did, over many years and in depth, and with great compassion for the victims, whether local to southern California or in remote Eskimo villages, where nearly every young man in each of the towns Bill reported from had been molested by a Catholic priest.

At the end of his reporting—which spanned several years and other various and sundry church and parachurch scandals—Bill was one very cynical agnostic. When he came on my show to discuss his book and his faith train wreck, Carol heard him and recalled that Bud knew both Bill and me. Through Bud, she set up a meeting for Jan and me to see about rekindling Bill's internal spiritual fire.

So out of the blue, Jan Janura showed up on my back porch to smoke a cigar and drink some wine and talk about getting Bill to Montana, which happened. What has happened to Bill since is another story, not my own, and he will tell it sometime, but what I can tell you is that Jan became my fast friend even though I hate to fish, and the guides at the Beartooth Lodge on the Madison hate me to fish as much as I hate to try. But I sure enjoy being with Jan.

Thus an encouragement machine was installed in my life. I already had one, my wonderful wife, and another in Bud and a third in Coach Jerry, more about whom later. But as wonderful and necessary as encouragement from a spouse is, it is not the same as third-party encouragement. When you speak or write words of encouragement to someone outside your family, you are kindling their self-esteem. (Ask yourself right now, who is the encouragement machine in your life? Then ask for whom are you that machine?)

Self-esteem is a fascinating quality. Too much makes a man or a woman at least a bore and perhaps even a narcissist. Too little turns him or her into an insecure shadow of a fully developed adult. The right amount, though—that is a wonderful thing. And also a precious, passing thing, like gas in the tank of a moving car. It needs to be refilled, mostly by self-generation and the right appraisal of efforts undertaken and jobs well done. This is what Arthur Brooks, the president of the country's most influential think tank, the American Enterprise Institute, calls "earned success." Earned success brings about self-esteem, but encouragement provides a valuable assist in creating and replenishing that self-esteem.

Do you think Sinatra, the Beatles, Bette Midler, Lady Gaga, or the next big thing were indifferent to encouragement? Certainly they relished it when they were not yet superstars.

How do I know that? Because I have interviewed a lot of great entertainers and read their memoirs, and all of them—among them Andy Williams, Carol Burnett, Dick Van Dyke—know and crucially name the people who thought they had the stuff of stardom when they were far from it, who gave them a break, who, in a word, encouraged them.

We tend to think encouragement matters less and less as we get older, but it matters more and more as the number of people in the sort of relationship capable of delivering that encouragement grows smaller.

It matters in an obvious way in the aftermath of defeat or failure, as when a friend has lost a job or a young person has been cut from a team or denied admission to a college or a grad school. It matters to every writer who has ever written a book, and to every producer, director, and actor who has worked the stage or screen, small or big. Musicians, chefs, preachers, and athletes all need encouragement. But so do accountants and bus drivers, stay-at-home moms and dads, and every teacher in the world. "You are very good at what you do" is gold.

But not wholly like gold because you have a limitless commodity of it at hand, as does every single person. At every moment of every day there is an opportunity to encourage if an e-mail can be sent or a comment made. You don't even need to know the person you are encouraging. If you observe a worthy thing—any job well done or action deserving of praise—you are empowered to say so.

The people most in need of encouragement in your life are those you are most closely connected to, including spouse, children, and parents. (I didn't say above that a spouse's encouragement wasn't a necessity, just that it wasn't sufficient in itself.) You can throw kindling on that fire of self-esteem every day, and you should.

I think the most important encouragement I have ever witnessed was that given by my wife to our daughter in the days after our first granddaughter was born. Our daughter was exhausted from the delivery, overwhelmed by the neediness of the baby, full to overflowing with new hormones and emotions, and though supported by a great husband and new dad, she needed to hear the truth from someone who had truly "been there and done that": she was doing a great job and would be a great mom. And she has been a terrific mom and will continue to be. That's what Betsy told her would be the case then, and that's what every new mom needs to hear and to continue to hear. I am sorry for those who don't have their own moms to hear it from. I hope others will whisper encouragement in their ears as nurses and doctors and neighbors so often do.

Experienced teachers encourage new men and women at the front of the classrooms. Those senior teachers owe the younger ones no gratitude, but they do provide great pick-me-ups after long first-times around the block. Older coaches do the same for younger ones.

In his book *Work Hard. Be Nice.*, *Washington Post* reporter Jay Mathews tells the story of two out-of-their-depth and over-whelmed Teach for America rookies from the Ivy League who were thrown with little preparation into a tough inner-city Houston school. I will talk about these young men and what they started later in this book, but understand now that they were taken under the wing of an experienced African American woman used to the rough environment, who was skilled in pro-ducing achieving students. She taught these rookie teachers and, most important, kept their spirits up. Because of her encour-agement, the rookies were later able to start a brand of charter school—KIPP or "Knowledge Is Power Program"—which has swept across the country revitalizing neighborhoods and pro-viding genuine education to tens of thousands of students who would not otherwise have had it. All because one veteran teacher encouraged two rookies.

Chances are that someone encouraged you as a youth, as a young adult, and perhaps as a senior citizen. If that happened, it is likelier that you are yourself an encourager. If not, it is easier to understand why you haven't been giving away encouragement. It is a learned behavior.

Over and over again I have found that the people I most admire for the quality of their lives have been inveterate encouragers of others, always looking to push, prod, compliment, or cajole.

If you are not experienced in this habit, here's a suggestion:

Start with the next complete stranger you encounter across a counter, whether at Starbucks, a movie theater, or an airline check-in. As you wait for your service, imagine what the best thing you could say to that individual could be, what might possibly be remembered later that day after they are home and off their feet, a recollection that would redeem a hard day or make a good one even better. "You are very good at this job," is the most obvious of all candidates. Give it a whirl.

Encouragement doesn't require sainthood or even near-sainthood, just an eye for accomplishment and/or effort and a willingness to remark upon it in a habitual, indiscriminate but truthful fashion.

Have you encouraged anyone today? Do you recall how they reacted to that word? Nothing is for sure, but genuine encouragement is almost everywhere and every time met with gratitude and joy. Sometimes sheepish. Sometimes embarrassed. But rarely insincere.

THE
SECOND
GIFT

ENERGY

Whatever your hand finds to do, do it with your might.

—THE BOOK OF ECCLESIASTES

LOUIS ZAMPERINI VANISHED FROM THE PUBLIC'S MIND for more than sixty years. The Olympian and World War II hero had come back from captivity to national acclaim, then to eclipse and a nasty fall into alcoholic despair. Then, as told by the amazing Laura Hillenbrand in *Unbroken*, Zamperini was back on the front pages of every paper and in the collective consciousness of a first shocked, then surprised and admiring country.

Years before *Unbroken* soared to the top of the best-seller list, my friend Linda Roberts had given me an autographed copy of Zamperini's memoir, *Devil at My Heels*. Linda and her husband, Mark Roberts (theologian, author, and my dear friend and pastor before he decamped to Texas), had known Louie as a fixture at Hollywood Presbyterian Church where Mark's mom had been on staff for years and where Mark began his pastoral career after his undergraduate and graduate studies at Harvard.

Linda and Mark are the sort of deeply grounded Christian friends that everyone should have, and to whom everyone should listen. But when Linda suggested I read Louie's memoir, I didn't. So I was as surprised as the next person when his extraordinary story of heroism, endurance, and grace became as well known as the latest reality show star.

I reached out to Louie through Olympian John Naber who, as a fellow USC Trojan, was helping him navigate the rush of media invites Louie received after *Unbroken* appeared. Despite my love of Trojan bashing on air, the always-amiable Naber worked out a date with Louie, and the two arrived at my Orange County studio for an interview.

I asked my producer, Duane Patterson, to meet them in the parking lot and show them the way to the elevator. My studio is usually reached by a double flight of stairs, but Zamperini was over ninety, and I assumed—bad thing for a journalist—that he'd need the elevator. But no, Louie fairly leapt from the car, waved off Duane's directions, and bounded up the stairs, bursting into a studio that included my wife, my sister-in-law Jody, my niece Anne, and a few others. He embraced them all with hugs and handshakes and crashed into the studio itself with a hearty "Let's go"—which we did, live and on air for an hour. Then he was up, out, down the stairs, and off to a book signing for more than a thousand people, through which he sat cheerful and animated, a wonder and an inspiration.

Louie Zamperini embodied the gift of energy that day, an

amazing flow of life and love that transformed every room into which he walked and person with whom he talked. He has the gift of energy, and he gives it away.

For a decade, I cohosted a nightly news and public affairs show for the Los Angeles PBS affiliate, KCET. The program was titled *Life and Times*, and my on-air colleagues included Patt Morrison, Kerman Maddox, and Ruebén Martinez. It was essentially a talking heads show of the sort that are common now on Fox News and MSNBC, but which didn't exist outside of the weekends in 1992.

Our senior producer was (and remains) an amazingly talented television professional, Martin Burns. From my first show to my last—I left the series when my radio show moved to the afternoon drive slot in 2002—Martin would crouch before the panel just as the green light was about to flash and say, "Energy." He knew energy in the hosts was the secret to good television. He may also have known it to be the secret to nearly everything that needs doing.

Energy is simply that, and needs no definition. It's the means to any end, and it can be given away in amazing amounts. Its opposite, lethargy, is just as easy to spot and carries exactly the opposite impact of energy.

People with energy energize others. Proximity is all it takes, which is a good reminder to stay close to the energetic. In *Mere Christianity*, C. S. Lewis supplied the image of a fountain of energy. "If you are close to it, the spray will wet you," he said, "if you are not, you will remain dry."

I have been a runner for years now, though these days a slower, heavier runner than in my speedier days in the early eighties. (Amazed youngsters cannot believe my personal best of 3:13:42 in the 1983 Marine Corps Marathon, but look it up, o ye of little faith.) Two of the reasons I still get up and get out there are two guys—older than I am by more than a few years— whom I see on my regular rounds, one fellow with a big white mustache in my neighborhood, and the other invariably wearing a Purdue T-shirt down by the Huntington Beach pier. Both men cannot be said to be gliding anymore than I am, but both seem to be enjoying themselves and are motoring along as they have been for years and years. Their commitment, their example, their energy inspire me. They are, I think, at least a decade ahead of me in years, so I tell myself that as long as they are out there, I have at least ten years of morning runs ahead of me. They have kept their energy for running going. So can I.

Nowhere is the principle of energy transfer more obvious than in sports and in teaching. A player of any game at any time who doesn't bring his or her energy with them is an albatross on the team and a ticket to losing. All the talent in the world cannot compensate for the drive that accompanies an energetic effort. Similarly, I can tell if learning is underway in a classroom simply by the amount of energy on display at the front of the room.

"Energy and persistence alter all things," said Benjamin Franklin. The love of living at full speed and with full commitment transforms every field of endeavor.

In October 2012, I arrived in Dallas to moderate a "debate" between James Carville and his wife, Mary Matalin, before a group of successful trial lawyers—the members of the Products Liability Advisory Council. I'm no trial lawyer, but my law partner and very successful defense counsel and PLAC member, Gary Wolensky, wrangled me into the gig. The biggest problem was not my lack of expertise in products liability matters. Hugh

Young, who captains the council, is both a high achiever and something of a sadist: he scheduled the kickoff breakfast-debate for 7:30 a.m., on the morning after the first presidential debate between Barack Obama and Mitt Romney, which had been held in Denver and featured a memorable thrashing of the president by the governor.

After broadcasting a special six-hour show the evening before, I showed up bleary-eyed and wondering if Carville would even make it to the event. James had been the featured analyst on CNN as late as I had been on radio—and he had to fly into Dallas from Denver, the site of the presidential debate, that morning.

Carville did, of course, arrive and, fortified by coffee, put on his full game face and launched into one of the very best back-and-forths that I have ever heard on what all the country had just seen, including a memorable soliloquy on how hard—really and truly hard—it is to endure a presidential race. Mary Matalin, the other half of the best platform duo in all America, no doubt helped him turn in this power performance, giving him energy as she kept up an amazing stream of anecdote, insight, and humor.

When we exited the stage I paused to thank them both for a great ninety minutes, and told James I particularly appreciated how much game he brought after such a late night and a hurried trip south.

"If you can't play hurt, don't play the game," he drawled with that signature smile.

Carville's ferocious energy at sixty-eight was something to behold, but I see it in many people as old and older every day, just as I see lethargy in youngsters every day. It is a puzzle as to who decides to live with energy and who doesn't, but my belief is that either way, it is a choice.

That's right. With very few exceptions having to do with underlying medical conditions, the amount of energy anyone brings to any undertaking, from painting a room to running for office, from preaching a sermon to mowing a lawn—it is all a choice. Yes, fatigue sets in. And yes, the events of a day or week can grind and slow you down, but the willingness to charge is a choice. It is a learned behavior. And it can be taught if it is modeled.

My previous chapter on encouragement and my next chapter on enthusiasm make similar points, but the overlaps shouldn't obscure things here. Encouragement can be offered from a deathbed, indeed from beyond the grave, and enthusiasm is a particular thing directed at particular enterprises. But not energy. Energy is what the living give to the living. Every parent knows this. Every teacher and every coach.

Tackling tasks in a straightforward, let's-get-this-done, energetic way sets a powerful example, one that teenagers especially seem immune to, but are not. They see and absorb everything, and if they are immersed in lethargy they will become lethargic. Their rapidly growing bodies leave them fatigued and in need of lots of sack time, but it is every parent's, teacher's, and coach's job to keep their own motors running so that the example of life tackled at full speed is seen.

Both of my sons were blessed by a water polo coach who ran early—early—morning practices and weights in-season and out, always there himself, always on time. Matt Campbell had a huge impact on them and on hundreds of other boys in those crucial years, by demonstrating what it meant to do a job day in and day out with the energy and commitment necessary to do it well.

This kind of modeling is more important now than ever, the

gift more valuable than ever. Brad McCoy is the father of NFL quarterback Colt McCoy, and was one of the most successful high school football coaches in Texas when he retired to go into executive coaching. I interviewed him about *Growing Up Colt*, a book he coauthored with his son. He reflected on the number of young men in America—millions and millions and more every year—without any man in their home lives, much less their dads. For these boys, he argued, coaches had gone from important figures to crucial, indeed indispensable, keys to their entire lives. Nowhere is this truer than in this area of modeling energy and the attitude it takes to turn it on, the simple but crucial act of will to be fully involved in the task at hand.

If you read biographies of Winston Churchill—and I hope you do—it's impossible to miss his energy. William Manchester and Paul Reid capture it in their three-volume biography *The Last Lion*. It practically leaps from the page. It's the same with Sir Martin Gilbert's vast official biography, as well as every other treatment of the greatest man of the twentieth century.

Churchill was almost always full of a ferocious, incomprehensible energy, one that swallowed up entire subjects and careers and reordered them into a sprawling, exuberant life force that single-handedly rallied Great Britain from its deathbed and led the West to victory over evil in the form of Hitler and Imperial Japan. His energy had for years been a source of scorn among his peers in the British upper class, but when it counted, when everything hung in the balance, the man needed by the world, by history, by everything good and honorable was sixty-five years old and powerfully energized, keeping hours and a pace that astonished even as it transformed a near-defeated nation.

Read Manchester's and Reid's trilogy to catch a spark of greatness and a model of life lived at the speed for which it was intended. You will set yourself on fire—and those around you as well—if you absorb that life lesson.

THE
THIRD
GIFT

ENTHUSIASM

Be ... fervent in spirit.

—THE EPISTLE TO THE ROMANS

AS A SERIAL ENTHUSIAST, I AM ALWAYS DRAWN TO reruns of the old television show *Malcolm in the Middle* and every new episode of *Modern Family*. Both enormously successful sitcoms featured serial enthusiasts: Hal, the dad in *Malcolm*, played by Bryan Cranston, and Phil, the dad in *MF,* played by Ty Burrell. They make everyone laugh, but especially those of us who are drawn to new interests and temporary passions by a mixture of curiosity and ADHD.

Lots of folks know the line, "Go big or go home." For serial enthusiasts, it is better to say, "Dive deep, but you'll be out of the water shortly."

Serial enthusiasm is a counterpart to the sustained enthusiasm that makes for wonderfully committed hobbyists. I am definitely in the former category. Not for me are the joys of collecting stamps, butterflies, or political memorabilia, nor the search for the perfect golf swing that has followed many a life from near cradle to grave.

I have been married for thirty-one wonderful years, and one of the secrets to happy marriage is clearly indulging a spouse's flights of interest, whether serial or sustained. The Fetching Mrs. Hewitt has always been a star in this regard. A happy life requires diversions. Our passion about our work and our family is an aspect of the well-lived life; but passion about pastimes is crucial to mental and physical health.

The enthusiasm that lubricates life is the most mysterious of virtues. I have seen it often but cannot with anything approaching certainty tell you where it comes from. But when I pass a cyclist in bright Lycra, or a marathoner-in-training struggling through one of many long runs, or a volunteer on a political campaign, or a Bible study group that has been meeting for decades, I know that enthusiasm prompted and sustains their commitment.

So many of my guests over the years have displayed this essential quality of happy living: Andrew Breitbart, Arianna Huffington, Larry O'Connor, Guy Benson, Richard Dreyfuss, Willie Brown, James Lileks, Ken Mehlman, Reince Priebus, "Dan the Skimmer Target" and "Dan the Sub Man" (two of my regular callers, both Navy vets), Mark Steyn, Fred Barnes, and Eric Metaxas—to name just a few.

James Lileks has been a guest on my radio show for as long as I can recall, and before then I was reading his daily "Bleat" at Lileks.com. A columnist for the *Minneapolis Star Tribune* and for *National Review*, James is the rare character who combines both serial and focused enthusiasm. His deep dives into various and many fascinating areas—architecture, matchbooks, the music of the home front during WWII, *Star Trek*, and noir film—flow effortlessly into his website and his novels and nonfiction work. Some of his passions become part of his income stream (such as his book *The Gallery of Regrettable Food*), but he would have collected the images and recipes for some of the hideous dishes of the fifties even if they had not been intended for book form. It's what Lileks does. And that is why he's so happy, and his happiness explodes when he's on the air. He is endlessly interesting to listeners, which is why I welcome him weekly. Enthusiasm attracts.

As does the amazing Mark Steyn. Yes, Steyn is a prolific, pointed, and wickedly funny purveyor of ideas. But he is also an omnivore of everything. His grasp of Broadway and song, for example, amazes everyone, as does his command of the peculiarities of many, many nonpolitical lives. For years the *Atlantic* commissioned Steyn to write end-of-the-issue obituaries of various interesting though often-forgotten people, like "Luft, Artie Shaw, Ronald Reagan, the Reverend Canaan Banana, and a gaggle of other towering figures, scurvy lowlifes, and all points in between." I quote the blurb from Mark's website, SteynOnline.com. All those obits—plus entries for Tupac Shakur, the Princess of Wales, Bob Hope, Madame Chiang Kai-shek, and the man who created Cool Whip—are collected in Steyn's book *Passing Parade*.

Sadly, another of my favorite enthusiasts and regular radio guests is no longer with us. Andrew Breitbart, loved by his friends, fanatically hated by his opponents, was as great an enthusiast as I have ever met. No matter when we sat down together (our friend

Jude the musician first brought him to my studio) or talked over the air, the ground we covered was vast, including his proclivity for New Wave music. Andrew moved in enormous jumps, like John Carter on the new planet in the horrific movie by the same name. By the end of a sentence, he was on a different continent from the one on which he started. He moved at the speed of light, assessing, judging, and moving on.

People grieved Andrew's early and untimely death because he was a sincere friend to so many. How was that possible? He was genuinely interested in and enthusiastic about what they did. He was genuinely interested, not cocktail party interested. He wanted to go into a bar and sit and chat and chat and chat. He was even interested in his enemies, to the point of retweeting the horrible things they wrote about him—a practice I disagreed with and urged him to abandon. I lost that battle.

That was Andrew's way, to engage, probe, puzzle, decide— and then announce it all in public. Every day, all day, he was driven by an enthusiasm for the collision between left and right and powered by his endless curiosity about the lives of others.

There are many others like him. Andrew's protégé Larry O'Connor shares this love of everything and deep curiosity backed by a willingness to explore and learn. It is what makes most talk show hosts good at what they do. Was anyone ever more interested in more topics than William F. Buckley, as good at exploring all sorts of points of view and lifestyles as the greatest editorialist of the second half of the American Century?

The late Vince Flynn, who died at the very young age of forty-seven after soaring again and again to the top of every best-seller list, was another human perpetual motion machine, imbuing his lead character Mitch Rapp with the same intensity and energy that Vince brought to every interview, book tour, and especially as his friends and family attested after his death, to those around him whom he loved most.

The left has serial enthusiasts too. My favorite is Richard Dreyfuss, and the Academy Award–winning actor has a unique place in my ten-thousand-plus interviews. Dreyfuss is the only subject I ever interviewed who used up all the television tape my crew had brought along.

When I worked for the Los Angeles PBS affiliate from 1992 to 2002, I would occasionally do long form sit-downs with actors and directors, from Oliver Stone to Charlton Heston, from Sydney Pollack to Anthony Minghella. The producer for such shoots was either Martin Burns or Saul Gonzales. Both are extraordinarily skilled pros, and the crews were always ready and prepped to roll.

But with Dreyfuss we talked for three hours and simply ran out of tape. Gone. Why? Because he was fascinating, loved politics, loved to argue, had watched my show for years and knew I was a conservative but was willing to debate rather than dictate, and especially because he was willing to talk expansively about his many ups and downs, his many interests—yes, musical instruments and high school teaching—and, of course, his movies. Dreyfuss has lived his life as an enthusiast for people and passions (and for a time, sadly, for drugs, from which he has recovered). His recounting of his life was thus an endless series of fascinating stories.

His Oscar? *The Goodbye Girl.* C'mon, you were thinking *Close Encounters* or *Mr. Holland's Opus*, right? He was nominated for the latter.

The Dreyfuss interview remains one of my favorites, but also up there is a memorable sit-down I had with Willie Brown, and for the same reason. Brown is an epic figure in California political history. He served thirty years in the California Assembly, including fifteen years as its Speaker, the longest run as Speaker ever, and one that will not likely ever be equaled because of the adoption of term limits. Willie Brown went on to serve two terms as mayor of San Francisco, and can still be counted on to be the funniest, most engaging man in the room, no matter how crowded it is. And the best dressed.

When I interviewed him and asked what he loved most about his job—this was near the end of his long, long (and to GOPers seemingly endless) run as de facto king of the state—he replied, "Hugh, I must admit that sometimes I simply love the raw exercise of power." Ah, candor, the most wonderful of things for an interviewer. And candor from a man at the top of his power? Priceless.

Willie was priceless because he loved every minute of every day as far as anyone who was watching could tell. Why? In the same interview he told me about growing up in a dirt-floor shack in Texas, raised by his grandmother in grinding poverty. Willie Brown came from nowhere to San Francisco, among the most beautiful places in the world, and he was going to live life with enthusiasm and abandon. Like Breitbart, like Dreyfuss, like Steyn and Lileks and so many others.

Readers might think that fame is required to have this gift, but it isn't. Far from it, and many famous people are really quite dull upon examination. (I have suffered through some very awkward interviews with very famous people who are, well, as interesting as cement without initials or footprints.) They are enthusiastic about themselves but not much else. Self-absorption is never interesting and is a sort of malignant enthusiasm that can be shared only partially, and then only by the craven.

When in the course of a radio show I encounter something with which I am wholly unfamiliar—orchids, snow boarding, bridge—I simply call out to my audience for an assist and in they come from the far corners of the country, a legion of smart and experienced people who know a thing or two about what I need to know.

Dan the Sub Man and Dan the Skimmer Target are two long-time callers from Phoenix who help me out of many a naval jam. Railroads? Oh, the number of people fascinated by trains! Gardening? Well, I can begin with the Fetching Mrs. Hewitt's closest friend, her cousin Diana; but as far and wide as is the earth there are people who not only tend it but are willing to talk endlessly and with genuine passion to those of us who cannot tell weed from healthy blade.

My passion for running—once fast, now slowly—is shared by as many people as you see gliding or trundling by. I caught this bug in 1982, and thirty years and thirty additional pounds later I am still at it, though far off my best times. (Did I mention my personal best of 3:13 in the 1983 Marine Corps Marathon? Oh, I did? Vanity, all is vanity.) I dream of getting back under four hours before the end of my days on this earth.

There is a book, a wonderful book about running, which is really about enthusiasm, and whether or not you have run a quarter mile in your life or tens of thousands, you ought to take it in as an example of what enthusiasm can do to a life, both good and bad. *Born to Run: A Hidden Tribe, Superathletes, and the Greatest Race the World Has Never Seen* is an amazing work by Christopher McDougall, a book that recounts the world of ultramarathoners both domestic and foreign, and the not easily studied Tarahumara tribe in Mexico who are ultramarathoners.

I point you to this book because it is of that small class that could conceivably change your life by inspiring you to change your lifestyle. Jim Fixx did that for me in the seventies with *The Book of Running*. Fixx, who later died of a congenital heart defect, inspired millions with his enthusiasm and launched the running boom of that era, which has spread and spread and spread. Today, not far from where I live, there is a ministry to homeless people that begins with their lacing on used running shoes. For them it is a way back from lost lives, through substitutionary habits about which they grow, yes, enthusiastic.

How to share this gift, this capacity to be engaged and changed by new things, pastimes, discoveries? Enthusiasm is, as the cliché goes, contagious. But like colds, it requires contact; and some folks do their best to avoid infection. This is where judiciousness comes in.

Never ask a friend to dive deep with you. Ask him or her to come to the shore once or twice to watch. A marathoner can take a friend for a mile walk-jog along a favorite path, a horseman a newbie for a first ride, a hunter a city boy for an early-morning foray.

Lend your favorite books. Better, give them; no one ever returns books anyway. Give tickets to the opera or symphony to friends who weren't expecting them. Plan a road trip to obscure sites of obscure historic anomalies. (I once drove my trusting, unsuspecting sons to the very edge of Ohio, where on State Route 128 in North Bend, along the banks of the famed river, is the William Henry Harrison Tomb State Memorial. It has a parking lot for two vehicles. Ours was the only one.)

Most of the time these efforts to share passion will be as unrequited as a seventh-grade crush. But when the click and the connection is made and the passion passed, the arc of a life changes, and it changes for the good, for the very great good.

This is the essence of evangelization, by the way. The passing to others of the deep enthusiasm for the truth of the gospel works best not by didactic teaching, though teaching has its place, but by exuberant faith and relational ministry. As we live and celebrate our faith, people around us see and inquire, absorb, and multiply that faith.

As he read the draft of this chapter, my friend (and this book's editor) Joel Miller suggested that I was veering close to a discussion of *ascesis* (self-discipline). That might strike you as strange. What does self-discipline have to do with enthusiasm? But Joel pointed me to this passage in Pope Benedict XVI's book *The Spirit of the Liturgy*:

> The body must be trained, so to speak, for the resurrection. Let us remember incidentally that the unfashionable word *askēsis* can be simply translated into English as "training." Nowadays we train with enthusiasm, perseverance, and great renunciation for many different purposes—why do we not train ourselves for God and his Kingdom?

You cannot successfully train for any skill, profession, hobby, or calling for which a deep enthusiasm does not already exist. With enthusiasm, however, almost any hardship in training can be endured and difficulties surmounted so that we grow in expertise. So it is with every sport, every intellectual pastime, and our faith lives—maybe especially our faith lives.

Not long ago a group of adults from my Presbyterian church embarked on a two-week trip to South Africa, to the most desperately poor areas of the country, where our church had long sent aid to a few churches, food stations, and schools. Our pastor asked mostly first-time missionaries to go, folks like investors, lawyers, and accountants.

The seven who went returned transfigured and alive with an enthusiasm for what could still be done, not just for what had been done. As I write this they are busy planning a trip of about seventy of us to the same place. Did you follow that math? From seven to seventy. Enthusiasm is exponential. I told one of the seven, my pal Steve Thames, that he was coming dangerously close to persuading my wife to join him and his wonderful wife, Monica, on a future trip that would be empty of the sort of creature comforts I crave. Thus does enthusiasm work.

This is a common tale from many churches, not often told outside of their walls but as incredibly important to the world as it is to the individuals. This is how enthusiasm travels and transforms at its highest level, but it works for every passion and for every person given persistence and patience.

EMPATHY

To him who is afflicted, kindness should be shown by his friend.

—THE BOOK OF JOB

YEARS AGO I HOSTED A SERIES FOR PBS TITLED *Searching for God in America.* It aired in the summer of 1996, and consisted of half-hour conversations with key religious leaders on the big questions.

The show itself had been birthed in panic a year and a half earlier when Republicans under the leadership of Newt Gingrich had seized the House in the elections of 1994. No one saw that coming, and as a new GOP and conservative leadership took control of the House purse strings, PBS was not alone in suddenly wanting to appear to be far more ideologically balanced than it in fact was.

In 1994 I was one of the very few conservatives with an on-air role anywhere in the PBS system. As noted earlier, I worked then as the host of a nightly news and public affairs program called *Life and Times* for KCET. My station president, the wonderful Bill Kobin, got a call from DC: Would Hewitt be interested in hosting a national show? I instantly figured out that Operation Balance-the-Window-Dressing was underway. I said yes, provided the show could be about faith.

At that time there was nothing in that category. This was before the explosion of cable, and before anyone started thinking that faith was a vibrant topic for television. Some huddling and hemming and hawing ensued, along with much negotiation over content. But when my senior producer Martin Burns and I set out on our eight extended taping sessions with eight "big guns" of faith, we were in for a rare and very enriching experience.

The eight guests were Evangelical, Mormon, Jewish, Catholic, Sufi Muslim, and Buddhist: Charles Colson, Rabbi Harold Kushner, Dr. Roberta Hestenes, Pastor Cecil Murray, Professor Seyyed Hossein Nasr, Elder Neal Maxwell, Father Thomas Keating, and finally the Dalai Lama. It took four months to film all the interviews. We would fly off for a day or two of long, taped conversations about God, life, death, happiness, and prayer with these eight individuals. We filmed Father Keating in his austere monastery in the Rockies in the middle of winter, His Holiness at a Buddhist gathering in the Ritz-Carlton in Buckhead outside of Atlanta, Elder Maxwell at Brigham Young's Beehive House in Salt Lake City.

I took a great deal away from this series, but there's one insight I didn't realize at the time. Each of these men and Dr. Hestenes had great capacity for empathy, and that was because each had suffered greatly. Their suffering had not deformed them, but rather had formed them into complex carriers of love and understanding.

These are not soft people. The opposite in fact. The Dalai Lama quite literally fled through mountain passes to escape the Communist Chinese after Mao ordered the Red Army to invade and enslave Tibet. Neal Maxwell stormed the beaches at Iwo Jima, and Chuck Colson was a Marine, a ruthless White House aide, and a survivor of prison who himself walked the Bible into the hardest, most dangerous prisons on the planet.

Sayyed Hussein Nasr fled the religious police of revolutionary Iran. Father Keating led a monk's life of work and self-denial. Murray stared down gang members and walked fearlessly through the Los Angeles riots and their aftermath. Roberta Hestenes held hundreds of Africa's children as they died of AIDS before we knew what the disease was, much less anything about its treatment. Rabbi Kushner went through the worst suffering of all: the slow loss of a child to a long and cruel disease.

Empathy is harder to describe than almost every other concept in this book. As a gift, it is superior to its cousins, sympathy and patience, so we should talk about the differences.

Empathy extends from identity. Anyone who gets to fifty-seven has experienced the sudden deaths of family and friends, and each of those deaths is a particular sort of loss. My parents and my wife's parents all died more than a decade ago, and each had a distinct checkout from this life and into the next: Alzheimer's, MS, breast cancer, and a sudden massive heart attack. Each of those losses equipped us with some hard experience that may make us more empathetic to others who experience the same thing. We are empathetic to people whose parents are sick or dying, but even more so to those whose moms and dads are battling Alzheimer's, multiple sclerosis, or breast cancer, or who are suddenly snatched away by a massive coronary.

Other hard experiences have increased my capacity to understand specific circumstances. I lost a college roommate in a car crash, a good friend of nearly forty years to liver cancer (Tom Fuentes, mentioned earlier), my pal and dentist of twenty years, Jerry Kushner, to ALS, and one of the greatest encouragers of my life, Coach Jerry Tardie, to a massive heart attack on Election Night 2012. (It appears from texting records that Jerry went to heaven just after Ohio was called for the president. Really.) With each searing experience comes the capacity for greater empathy generally, and some very particular circumstances with specificity.

Proximity also matters for the gift of empathy. Empathy is really only offered up close, but you and I can feel sympathy for people long dead or far, far away.

Two examples: I am certain some runners who crossed my path a few years back on my regular route in Huntington Beach, California, were surprised to see a grown man with ear phones stop, stand still, and wipe away abundant tears. I had been listening to Doris Kearns Goodwin's magnificent biography of Lincoln, *Team of Rivals*, and had just finished hearing the chapter recounting the president's loss of his beloved son Tad to fever, and how, surrounded by the awful, indeed indescribable, carnage of war, and burdened even more by a mentally unstable wife, he had to endure the loss of his great love, comfort, and joy. My sympathy for Lincoln, across the centuries, was profoundly moving to me, and I suspect to anyone who reads the account.

In a far more recent experience, I sat down to read Jake

Tapper's *The Outpost*. Tapper was, at the time he wrote the book, the ABC News senior White House correspondent and is now host of CNN's afternoon news program *The Lead*. Tapper is very able with a pen, so I expected to be informed but did not anticipate being so moved by his detailed account of the ultimately futile struggle to establish and defend a "combat outpost"—specifically Combat Outpost ("COP") Keating—in the mountains of Afghanistan's Nuristan province. The drama in the book is incredible and unrelenting. The losses of the American soldiers at COP Keating are all recounted with extraordinary detail and all are grief inducing. One in particular, the death of Lt. Col. Joe Fenty, was followed by a heartbreaking account of how his widow, caring for their newly born and only daughter, learned of her husband's death. Grief observed at this level must produce sympathy, or the reader has lost all humanity.

Tapper's book is one of those rare books of real art because it provokes deep, lasting sympathy in the reader. It is sympathy, though, not empathy, for I have not felt the loss of a son or daughter, husband or wife, father or mother to war.

I keep a memorial patch on my broadcast desk, that of USMC Lt. J. P. Blecksmith, lost in the second battle of Fallujah long ago, because I taught his sister, got to know his father, and have become friends with his friend and classmate and fellow Marine warrior Ronny Rowell. They have empathy for one another; I have sympathy for them all.

Similarly, when some younger friends of passing but serious acquaintance lost their little daughter, I could not imagine the grief. I could do no more than sympathize because that sorrow—numbered the worst by the wisest people—is beyond me. Sympathy, yes. Patience born out of sympathy if ever it were asked for, yes. But not empathy, not the deep under-standing that comes from shared experience.

You are qualified to give the gift of empathy to those with whom you share terrible experience, but that is mere qualifi-cation. Beyond identity of experience and proximity, empathy requires action. It is the gift of real understanding coupled with the concrete effort to help someone carry some specific burden. Empathy leads to the willingness to suffer alongside someone in a way that is far more profound and far more difficult than mere mourning. Mourning is necessary, a shared experience of grief, and something everyone ought to do whenever death or loss invades the lives of those around us. But the gift of empathy means a real willingness to go with the suffering people wherever they are and walk with them for as long as is required, to under-stand and to patiently endure with them all that their illness or loss entails.

When I think back to my eight guests—Colson, Nasr, Keating, and the others—it seems clear to me that what each of these people brought out of their trial was a great capacity to enter into, understand, and help carry the sufferings of oth-ers. Suffering taught them to live, to love, and to serve. Empathy alerted them how to do each, how to be present to the needs of those around them.

Of the many lessons I took from those conversations, the one I have quoted the most was Rabbi Kushner's bit of advice to those on the sidelines of suffering: "Show up and shut up." So simple. So short. So true. Empathy doesn't need many words or much volume. What it does require is presence.

It means showing up for a person whose experience you have shared in whole or part and saying to them, "I know a little of what you are going through and am available to help you as you want help."

This last part is important, so I want to repeat it slowly: As. You. Want. Help.

Empathy is a wonderful gift to give if it is empathy you want to give, and not sympathy that you want to receive. How many people who are already burdened find themselves on the receiving end of stories about how the teller has gone through the same thing, only perhaps a little worse for a lot longer, or a lot worse for far longer, or not only this, but also that and that and that? The offer of faux empathy is in fact the curtain-raising cue on the often rehearsed stories of personal suffering.

"Show up," the rabbi said, "and shut up."

The gift of quiet, advice-free companionship in the midst of suffering is a gift of the highest order. There is no down side to advice if it is sought, and much to be gained from it, if offered only when requested and then in the right amount. Shared experience makes the advice useful if it isn't overwhelming.

Empathy is an expensive, costly gift to give. It means reliving past sorrows and entering into new ones. I return to what I think is the hardest journey of all—that of a parent who has buried a child. I don't know how such moms and dads can bear to help others, how it cannot but open old and terrible wounds. But I know they do.

My friends who run the Injured Marine Semper Fi Fund have done amazing work in the years since their organization was founded after the invasion of Afghanistan in 2001. The Semper Fi Fund was begun by the spouses of Marines who'd gone off to fight wars, spouses who saw wounded Marines returning to a health care system that, while extraordinary in many ways, had enormous gaps. So the wives started raising money—to fly spouses and parents and girlfriends and boyfriends to their wounded Marines' sides, to pay for gas cards or hotel expenses, or to make up for lost paychecks when a parent had dropped everything to rush to the aid of a Marine who had lost one, two, three, or four limbs.

A decade later, these spouses had raised tens of millions of dollars and had given away $75 million of it in more than fifty thousand grants to more than ninety-five hundred Marines and their fellow soldiers, sailors, and airmen whom they had served alongside. From the latest in wheelchair technology to specially equipped athletic equipment to suitable housing, the Semper Fi Fund just gets it done, and with an overhead of less than 6 percent.

They know what they are doing, and they all say the same thing every Veterans Day and Memorial Day weekend when I host three-hour programs featuring some of the men and women they have assisted: by far the most inspiring people in the lives of wounded warriors outside of their families are the other wounded warriors who are further down the recovery road, already competing in the Marine Corps Marathon, or competing in some other sport, or begun upon a new career, or returned to active duty. When a double amputee sees a triple amputee thriving in life, passionate about whatever his pastime is, he can see himself on the other side of the chasm. The empathy—and sometimes the kicks in the butt—he receives from his fellow warriors drives him forward.

One of the most amazing accounts of such empathy was told to me on Memorial Day 2013 by a wounded Navy vet and his dad. The sailor—I think he had been a SEAL but, typically, was reticent to discuss his particular background—had lost a leg but had recovered to run and excel at marathons and triathalons. He and his dad first testified that the Semper Fi Fund had rallied to them in the early days of surgeries and recovery, but then they recounted how, in the aftermath of the Boston Marathon bombing, both had flown to the bedside of the victims who had lost limbs, so that the sailor could tell the patients that there was a lot of wonderful life ahead. The dad could tell the victims' parents the same thing.

That unique mission is what I'm getting at. Only they could have done that with as much effectiveness as they did.

This is what makes sponsors so crucial to the recovering alcoholics of AA. Whenever I have come across someone with an alcohol problem in the past twenty years, and that has been often, I tell him or her to find a meeting and at that meeting to find a sponsor. I have sent three different people to a fellow named Don, who has been sober for a very long time. A successful businessman, Don will spend as much time as is needed with any newcomer to AA. He knows what they are coping with, and he lets them know that and answers their questions.

When I am in New York City, I inevitably go to church either at St. Patrick's Cathedral, Tim Keller's Redeemer Presbyterian, Church of the Savior on Park Avenue and 38th, or to an open meeting at the AA clubhouse around the corner from News Corp. The sharing of faith is much more formalized at the first three, and I am familiar with the order of worship and the prayers. That isn't true at the open meetings of AA, where outsiders are welcomed, but not to speak: only to listen.

What I hear there are raw, hard stories of terrible suffering and hitting bottom, and also of redemption and recovery facilitated by someone who had compassion—empathy—for the drunk. Again and again and again, no matter how terrible the falls, the "old hands," the sponsors, would welcome and guide the newcomer.

Not always successfully. I have heard that story over and over again, but often enough and sometimes with spectacular success, at least for that day. The network shows on substance abuse are legion. I don't watch much television, but I hope they show the work of those people, those ordinary, wonderful people who are willing to throw in with the down-and-out and soon-to-be-dead-if-they-don't-change. AA is an empathy factory, turning out new champions of compassion every time a new attendee arrives and asks for help.

Empathy must be born out of experience. It's an action, not a feeling. Even if you aren't feeling empathetic, you can act as though you were. It is a habit of living, a very good habit, one that once developed will not easily wear out.

And you have a unique skill set in this area, one that cannot be replicated by others. It is the particular set of suffering you have been through, and there is someone waiting to hear from you on how that set is to be endured.

GOOD HUMOR

I know that nothing is better for them than to rejoice.

—THE BOOK OF ECCLESIASTES

MY PAL, THE WONDERFUL DENNIS PRAGER, IS AN ENDLESS source of good humor, and has for years offered a "Happiness Hour" once a week on his nationally syndicated radio show. As he says, "Happiness is a serious problem," and he even titled a book with that sentiment. (I expect Dennis and I will be out on a "happiness tour" in the years ahead since we both think this subject so crucial as to write books on it.) In a nutshell, Dennis believes it is necessary to wear happiness like a coat, as armor against whatever weather life throws at you. I think in this case "happiness" and "good humor" mean much the same thing—an attitude that reflects inner joy at being alive, or having a chance today to shine or love or be loved.

Good humor is a choice we make, and an attitude that is quickly communicated. "Good humor" is often accompanied by the adjective "infectious" for the simple reason that it quite obviously is. Mirth travels faster than a yawn—with the added bonus that it produces energy, not fatigue. It multiplies energy, reduces sadness, despair, and depression to very weakened states, and generally equips its bearers for great levels of productivity and achievement.

So why is it so rare? Take a few minutes and make a list of the people of "great good humor" of your acquaintance. Be honest. To whom does that high praise really belong?

In the world of radio one-offs—guests who appear once and only once—I have had some memorable good-humored interviewees. Not surprisingly, Julie Andrews and Dick Van Dyke were radiant with cheer over the air; and though I talked with them many years apart, they are joined in my head, and probably yours, as Mary Poppins and Bert, and thus have a head start in the good humor category. "Jolly Holiday" is just one of those tunes that everyone knows and that ought to bring at least a passing smile to faces.

Other good-humored guests have been pros at producing smiles, though comedians are the most dangerous of radio guests. Jeff Foxworthy, Tim Conway, Tracey Ullman, Harry Shearer—all have sat down for interviews that really weren't interviews but a series of cues for their monologues, which I had to interrupt occasionally to make commercial breaks. Foxworthy was the least destructive to my interview outline, but I told him up front that I had adopted a rule against interviewing comedians because of their tornado-like impact on production values. He did his best to stay on topic, which was his game show *The American Bible Challenge*. (Foxworthy is an amazing man of faith in addition to being the fellow who has sold the most comedy recordings in history, even more than Bill Cosby.)

Good humor professionals often aren't good-humored when the lights are down. Watch Billy Crystal's *Mr. Saturday Night* for a glimpse of that reality. In any event, good humor does not depend on the ability to tell a joke or deliver a punch line. Some of the worst storytellers in the world are blessed with fountains of good humor. Good humor is happiness of the soul made manifest on the face and in the voice of the bearer. It has little to do with timing.

Good humor has much to do with perspective—the long perspective—and flows from a sense of proportion, a knowledge that whatever the circumstances, they, too, shall pass. We are all headed to the same place at a different pace. I noted in the last chapter that I had the pleasure of interviewing His Holiness the Dalai Lama. Many, many people asked me, "What is he like?" confident that a three-hour conversation would provide a key to that question. I just tell everyone what I noticed at the time. The Dalai Lama was quite simply "a happy monk." He laughed throughout our long chat, even on the subject of death. He told me he spent time contemplating his own death every day.

Don't overlook the connection. My long-time radio guest and cruise colleague, Dr. David Allen White, spent a quarter century lecturing Naval Academy midshipmen on Shakespeare and other titans of literature before retiring to lecture beside me at sea. The good professor likes to remind everyone that every day they ought to think on four things: death, judgment, heaven, and hell.

Maybe these don't strike you as particularly humorous. Stay with me.

These are "The Four Last Things" in Catholic tradition, and their study is intended to lift the mind to the really important stuff. When the mind does that, it can appreciably increase good humor, because many of the pains and sorrows of the present quickly drop out of view. Even fresh or deep, deep wounds are eased against the backdrop of eternity. This is why I say good humor is a choice. Some may find such a perspective easier to attain than others, but we are able to change our outlook if we desire.

In addition to being a choice, good humor is a condition of repose, a basic happiness, a radiating joy. To me its connection to religious belief is obvious. Don't get me wrong. I have known a lot of gloomy people, plenty of whom were firmly convinced Christians. Isn't Scottish Presbyterian John Knox famously depicted as always scowling? Faith is no guarantee of good humor, but more often than not, faith does seem to be a necessary, if not sufficient, condition for good humor. Christopher Hitchens is an exception; he was marvelously happy most of the many dozens of times I spoke with him. But Richard Dawkins and Sam Harris, by contrast, seemed only to prove the rule in my few encounters with them.

When you have three children, as Betsy and I do, you learn that good humor is often a function of the clock. Our wonderful daughter, Diana, was not a morning person as a teenager, but was the soul of good humor late in the day, flowering with conversation and chatty asides as she plopped down in our bedroom chair just about the time we would have preferred to call it a day and turn out the lights.

Will, our second-born, is very much a morning person who almost always has had a welcoming smile early in the day, a product perhaps of years and years of early pool practices for water polo and swimming, and a crucial quality for the successful teacher he aspires to be. (If you are going to urge young men and women to plunge into a cold pool before 6:30 a.m., you must be the very model of good cheer. The same is true if you're asking sullen sophomores to try and get their arms around the drier patches of world history.)

Our youngest child, James, is like many youngest children, almost always amiable, a constant "How are you doing?" on his lips. Birth order is not destiny, but it is a pretty good map. And on that map, the youngest seem usually to live in the land of the contented and the cheery.

Truth be told, we are greatly blessed by the personalities of all our three children, though all three have been everything every child is—an enormous joy, a challenge, a source of great pride, and, rarely, the occasion of immense irritation if not anger. They are all young adults now, launched on their own lives. I will say more about them later, but in the good humor department, Betsy and I are three-for-three.

As adults, all three carry with them good humor and are ready to give it away. For this Betsy and I congratulate ourselves (though not too much; they each still have their days). We suspect that this attitude is the one most obviously imparted by day-to-day example, and my wife is the model of good cheer. She really is. An abundant joy marks her comings and goings, and I don't think any other friends and acquaintances would challenge this description. We all have our faults, but hers is not a lack of good humor.

The key question is whether good humor can be chosen, put on, pretended if it isn't really the way one is made. I am certain some readers are sneering right now, indignant at the idea that they choose not to be full of cheer, maybe even angry at the slightest suggestion that they are responsible for their God-given temperament. "Doesn't he know what I am up against? Doesn't he have a clue about what it means to have bills due, people around you sick, yourself ailing, children in terrible straits, an awful boss, a collapsing life, a crushing addiction, a silent God? Good humor, who is he kidding?"

I really do get this because I have put on the proverbial happy face all too many times when I felt like going full Vader. If you get to fifty-seven years with a wife of three-plus decades, three children, and many jobs and bosses, plus various assorted ups and downs, illnesses, and aging-then-dying parents, then you have been part of quite a few of life's bad jokes. But I don't think the inevitability of life's dramas and hard (sometimes devastating) knocks changes the basic question of whether or not to make the choice to greet it all with good cheer. When it comes to good cheer, we can all choose to try and be good actors, and even the least talented actor in the world can try and play this part.

It is possible to do so because we all know that change is not only possible, it is inevitable. We all know that people can make choices to change their circumstances so that even the worst day can, by small changes systematically repeated and repeated and repeated, be turned into a much happier, more productive future.

This is where it is good to know people's lives, to read biographies and to ask questions of everyone about their lives. (Do this when appropriate, not in the checkout line at Trader Joe's.) If, as is the case, every life lived has its best day and its worst day, knowledge of the worst days is an indescribably valuable bit of knowledge. If you really and truly know about the pits other people have been in and how they have emerged, you can get hope from that. If you meet people of great good cheer who have been in the pits of despair, you can figure a way out for yourself.

The very best path to good cheer is to practice it by simply smiling and inquiring after another's happiness. "How are you doing today? Great day, isn't it? Much to be done!" is the best gift you can give to anyone you meet, every single day, followed by empathy as needed and encouragement as warranted. But good cheer is the opening of the door. Who, after all, wants to begin a conversation with anyone carrying gloom on his face and whose every conversation begins with sourness and bile?

There are such people. You know them. Everyone knows them. They are for the most part genuinely unhappy and aggrieved, whether justifiably or not. They are frequently offended by just about everything and everyone.

It is a Christian's duty to walk with such people, but not all the time and not forever. To do so is to encourage their gloom, reward it, and deepen it. I am in difficult waters here, for I don't want to counsel a reader to abandon a troubled soul too quickly, but abandonment does have to be executed, and not rarely. Many people depend on those of good cheer, and the supply of cheer isn't endless. It cannot all be used up on one or a few, and it certainly must be reserved especially for family and for those who can use it most when they need it.

Good cheer is, in fact, exactly like charitable giving. You have some to give away. To whom will you give it?

With charitable giving, Betsy and I have always begun with our churches, and with ministries like Young Life and organizations that help our wounded veterans, like the Injured Marine Semper Fi Fund. There are other causes and charities we support, such as efforts begun by our friends to assist those who find themselves in various kinds of distress. But when the ability to give is exhausted, we stop. Mortgages must be paid and, until recently, college tuitions.

It is the same with the gift of good cheer. We know who needs it in our lives, and we are especially open to providing it to new people, strangers who cross our paths. With longtime family and friends, it is either easy or nearly impossible, the consequence of long years of call-and-answer drills, wherein the habits of good cheer offered-and-returned or offered-and-spurned are deeply ingrained patterns. With the former, no conscious effort is necessary. With the latter, none need be attempted, though cordiality is the residue of good cheer.

Thus the first moment I meet up with my radio colleague and pal Dennis Prager is always—always—a joy. For twenty years now, he has been greeting me with a hug he knows I hate. I am not, as I've often told my audience, a hugger. It's one reason I'm comfortable in Presbyterian churches. They are the houses of worship where I'm least likely to be hugged. That doesn't stop Dennis. It's probably God's plan to make up for all the hugs my personality has denied me over the years.

Dennis always brings a smile to my face. He is always alive with questions, instantly engaged in the conversation, an abundant high-energy power line lying on the ground ready to shock anyone who gets within its arc.

These days we see each other about four or five times a year, sometimes for extended periods of time, as when we tour as two members of a radio entourage heading from market to market on a promotional gig. We have often lectured together, and regularly do so now with a popular program, "Ask a Jew." It regularly sells out vast ballrooms, but the title sometimes makes people a bit uneasy.

"Do you object to 'Ask a Catholic'?" Dennis replied when an event coordinator raised this concern. He laughed and said, "I am a Jew! Hugh is asking me questions! Of course it is 'Ask a Jew'! What else can it be?" Pure Dennis, meeting bumps along the way with such force and abundant good humor that objections and obstacles melt away.

Dennis vibrates with good cheer. It is a life force within him—if I can use that New Age term with reference to the least New Age person I know. Dennis laughs and laughs and laughs, but can become serious in a second if the occasion demands. I want to be like Dennis. Good cheer overflowing, a "hale fellow well met" if there ever was one. A man of mirth who lights up every room he enters.

He can be copied, you know. Yes, he can. After all, good humor is a choice.

THE
SIXTH
GIFT

GRACIOUSNESS

Pursue peace with all people . . .

—The Epistle to the Hebrews

On the last Wednesday of his presidency, George W. Bush invited me and five other radio talk show hosts back to the Oval Office, ostensibly to thank us for support during the long years of his wartime presidency. We talked about several things, the solemnity of the surroundings lightened by his self-deprecating humor, until he finally told us why he had asked us back.

"Go easy on the next guy," he said. "It's a hard job. He'll get better at it. He'll have to. The country needs him to."

Surprised? I was but shouldn't have been. It was quintessential Bush, earnest and self-denying, capable of great surprises and deep feeling that were not often glimpsed by the public. He was the soul of graciousness, as many admirers realized then and more people realize today. However observers might assess the president's faults, a lack of graciousness is not among them.

The most enjoyable people are inevitably gracious folks. It's a quality easy to spot but impossibly hard to define. It is far more complicated than politeness, far more complex than the effortless display of fine manners and courtesy. Graciousness is the art of making people feel comfortable and included, appreciated and even admired. It is an elevating thing, the opposite of arrogance, the complement to humility.

If you have not read C. S. Lewis's space trilogy—*Out of the Silent Planet, Perelandra,* and *That Hideous Strength*—you will not be acquainted with NICE or Dr. Ransom, or the whole vast enterprise of Lewis's cosmology, all intended to drive home a major point about inclusiveness and graciousness versus exclusivity and cruelty. God's kingdom is wide open. We can be honest about this, right? It's not only wide open, it's full of His oddball assortment of apparently useless, positively off-putting, and very strange people. God is gracious and welcoming. (Those outcasts in the Lewis trilogy are the key to everything in the story, by the way, even as the marginal and the hopeless are the drivers of salvation in George R. R. Martin's epic fantasy *The Game of Thrones* and, of course, the hobbits Bilbo, Frodo, and Sam in Tolkien's *Lord of the Rings*. See a pattern there?)

Evil is just the opposite. Satan's world is a rigid hierarchy of unhappiness.

The foundation of graciousness is a recognition of radical equality, though not the sort that drove the French Revolution and then the Russian Revolution and the Khmer Rouge to their unspeakable acts of horror. This recognition is interior, a glimmer of reality that we can only behold in the heart. As Lewis said in his marvelous essay "The Weight of Glory":

> It is a serious thing to live in a society of possible gods and goddesses, to remember that the dullest most uninteresting person you talk to may one day be a creature which, if you saw it now, you would be strongly tempted to worship, or else a horror and a corruption such as you now meet, if at all, only in a nightmare. All day long we are, in some degree, helping each other to one or the other of these destinations. It is in the light of these overwhelming possibilities, it is with the awe and the circumspection proper to them, that we should conduct all of our dealings with one another, all friendships, all loves, all play, all politics. There are no *ordinary* people. You have never talked to a mere mortal. Nations, cultures, arts, civilizations— these are mortal, and their life is to ours as the life of a gnat. But it is immortals whom we joke with, work with, marry, snub, and exploit—immortal horrors or everlasting splendors.

There's another vital essay by Lewis, "The Inner Ring," that should be read in tandem with "The Weight of Glory." It is about the temptation of exclusivity, the sin of wanting to be "on the inside," privileged, elevated.

Lewis was professor of Medieval and Renaissance Literature at Cambridge University and was also a fellow of Magdalene College, Cambridge. "The Inner Ring" was the Memorial Lecture at King's College, University of London, in 1944. It was wartime, a time of many deaths, after years of many deaths and horrible sacrifices. It speaks volumes that Lewis chose to lecture on the soul-destroying practice of exclusivity at such a moment.

These two essays underscore the need for graciousness and its attribute, hospitality. To offer this gift is of profound importance.

Welcome someone into your world who is marginalized. No great plan of action is needed, just a simple decision to seek out and welcome an odd duck with few friends or an idiosyncrasy of some sort that makes it hard for him or her to flourish. Beyond that, embrace a rival or absolve an enemy and welcome him in as well. It looks like weakness and it feels like surrender, but it is graciousness.

Graciousness is practiced. It is intentional. It requires awareness of everyone in every day, from the person you turn in front of as you exit the street to the parking lot attendant, to every waiter or waitress in every restaurant. "Situational awareness" is one of those terms that military folk may or may not use, but which the actors who play the soldiers always use. Situational awareness of everyone in your life is the beginning of graciousness.

Children offer many occasions for pride. I think the greatest sources of pride for Betsy and me have been those occasions when someone told us of our kids' kindness to others, and all three have often been kind. Kindness to those who are struggling to find friends and acceptance is the most admirable thing, and in this they have all excelled. They are all adults now, in very different lives—a teacher, a politico, a spouse of a warrior—but in each of their lives they can and do welcome and include those who are not easy to welcome and include. Betsy and I must have done something right.

"The essence of good taste is to never be offended by bad

taste," is a famous saying, the origin of which I cannot recall. Ben Franklin said something similar: "He is not well bred who cannot bear ill breeding in others." Both bits of condensed wisdom point to the same command: be gracious.

The welcoming side of graciousness is captured in fiction by the character of Jim Prideaux in the John LeCarré novel *Tinker, Tailor, Soldier, Spy*. Prideaux is a cashiered spy—a killer in Her Majesty's service, wounded and discharged—who takes up retirement as a schoolteacher and befriends young Bill Roach, an outcast at the school, a victim of the bullying for which English boarding schools are legendary. Prideaux nicknames Roach "Jumbo," and slowly redeems his own life and the lad's. This is a minor part of a major work (in a genre that no one else has mastered like LeCarré), but it is a telling study of unnecessary kindness to a stranger that is the essence of graciousness. Read this book with an eye on that relationship and you'll glimpse one well-drawn case study of the gift being given. I marvel that LeCarré included this in his thriller, and appreciate that it is so central to understanding everyone, good and bad, in the tale.

One very gracious person—though you may find this completely at odds with his public persona—was Christopher Hitchens. He was my guest on the radio more than seventy times. I, a guest in his home for a most interesting dinner of picked-over chicken with an Iraqi exile, was not an intimate of Hitch's, but rather an acquaintance. He was a fellow with whom I was on the brink of friendship but not yet inside. Hitch was acerbic in debate and known for slicing and dicing his opponents. And ferocious as he might be, and hard and cutting, he was the soul of graciousness in person, especially with young people.

I accompanied him to Biola University—a lighthouse

institution for Christians on the West Coast—as the moderator of a debate on his book *God Is Not Great*, a debate done with accomplished Christian apologist William Lane Craig.

Hitch cracked up the audience of many thousands of students, parents, and the merely interested by beginning his remarks with, "Here I am, in the den of lambs." He stayed in the key of graciousness throughout, right through post-debate, late-night drinks with my then-intern Robby Stevenson. It was Robby's report that revealed another side of Hitchens, the kindly, curious, encouraging, and avuncular warhorse of the public intellectual lists, a man in full, unafraid to sit and chat with a college junior making his way in the world. (That college junior is now a United States Marine Corps lieutenant, and scheduled to be deployed at Camp Leatherneck in Afghanistan at the same time this book comes out.)

One of my favorite stories of graciousness also involved one of my interns. Each summer when my intern or interns arrive from college to learn a little about the real world of broadcasting, I assign them an impossible-to-book personality to pursue as an interview. I do this because it is good to learn how frustrating it can be to track down a guest; and since most people enter broadcasting through booking, it is a crash course in the very unglamorous side of the business, ranking just above answering the phones and weeding through the crazy people and the drunks as they search for the caller with something interesting to say.

Alley was a young woman fresh in from BYU, and "Vince Scully" popped into my head. Of course she wouldn't be able to book the legend. Scully was working, of course, and the last thing he needed to do was another hour of radio. After sixty-three years on air for the Dodgers, "the Voice of Summer" was about as close to broadcast deity as there is in this world. But Alley became a plague on the Dodgers' PR office, never relenting, always calling and e-mailing and following up—herself a model of graciousness. Her labor was, to her astonishment and mine, rewarded, and Vin Scully was scheduled.

Alley held her breath for at least an hour before Scully called to make the connection, and then as the interview began she feared he would be called away to Broadcasting Olympus after a minute or two, having made a gesture toward a young intern. But Vin Scully stayed on, taping an hour with me, an hour of pure Vin Scully artistry.*

Scully was, of course, gracious and wonderful, funny and winsome, charming and moving as we talked about his early life in the hardscrabble parts of New York City where his mom ran a tenement boarding house, about the nuns who wanted him to switch from left hand to right and the Jewish doctor who saved him, and about the desperate scramble for a first job and a break that he got after a memorable, freezing broadcast atop Fenway Park. As we reviewed some of his greatest calls—Henry Aaron's record breaker or Bill Buckner's heartbreaker—Scully's effortless mastery of the medium was on display, with the perfect phrasing and timing leading to an outcome that makes the radio insider smile with secret appreciation for the craftsman at work. For me, though, it was Scully's graciousness in agreeing to the persistent young intern's burning desire to bring home a big guest that impressed me most. A wise man, that Mr. Scully. Very gracious indeed.

---

* It's available online in the "Hughniverse," the archive of every hour of every radio show, and I encourage you to listen, as opposed to read the interview, since Scully's voice and timing is so wonderful, so absolutely perfect as only sixty-three years of practice could make it.

GRATITUDE

In everything give thanks...
—First Epistle to the Thessalonians

Rorke Denver is the retired Navy lieutenant commander and SEAL who played the role of Lt. Rorke in the 2012 hit movie *Act of Valor*, the extraordinary low-budget film that grossed nearly $75 million in theaters. It was made with the help of the United States Navy, and the key roles were filled by honest-to-God, active-duty SEALs. The producers decided—and the Navy surprisingly agreed—that it was easier to teach SEALs to act than actors to be SEALs. Not only did that prove to be true, but the willingness of the Navy to allow the filmmakers to follow real drills and film aboard carriers, submarines, and swift boats made the movie a trip to the front lines of battle that few civilian Americans have ever experienced.

Rorke retired from the Navy in early 2013 after a dozen years in the teams, the last four of which were spent supervising the training of would-be SEALs at the "Silver Strand" on Coronado near San Diego. He went about designing a new life as you might imagine a former SEAL would—methodically. That life included writing the best-selling book *Damn Few* and launching a speaking career that rewards every audience that hears him.

While writing *Damn Few*, Rorke called me to ask about the acknowledgments page, that part of most books wherein the author thanks the people who have helped him or her along the way.

"Put everyone on it," I told him immediately. "Anyone and everyone who has a legitimate claim on your gratitude for making the book happen."

This is the rule I have followed through a long line of books that stretch back to my first, *First Principles*, published long ago and far away in 1985 when I was still an assistant counsel in the Office of the White House Counsel. I had the time to write a book on political theory then because our office included a certain fellow named Roberts—now the chief justice of the United States Supreme Court. Our bosses knew which attorney to give the big issues to, and it wasn't me, so I had time to write. (The Chief Justice is indeed that smart, though his jump shot leaves a lot to be desired. Our office basketball team scored a solitary win, and only after importing ringers from the Department of Justice and the Government Accountability Office. White House lawyers and speechwriters not only could not jump, we couldn't shoot or play defense either. We were 1-9, and that one win came after a ringer was recruited who had played college ball.)

Since that 1985 book, I have turned out a regular stream of them and hope to keep doing so. It is what I do in addition to broadcasting, lawyering, and teaching. In every book I've included an acknowledgments page that tries to recognize everyone who has helped me with the project.

"No man but a blockhead ever wrote, except for money," Samuel Johnson famously said. But, of course, that isn't true, and it is especially not true in this age of digital publishing. But what money doesn't provide in way of motivation, vanity does, or at least a (usually) vain hope of influencing events. Again, here is the great Johnson, both on the ambition and its frustration:

> An assurance of unfading laurels, and immortal reputation, is the settled reciprocation of civility between amicable writers. To raise monuments more durable than brass, and more conspicuous than pyramids, has been long the common boast of literature; but among the innumerable architects that erect columns to themselves, far the greater part, either for want of durable materials, or of art to dispose them, see their edifices perish as they are towering to completion; and those few that for a while attract the eye of mankind are generally weak in the foundation, and soon sink by the saps of time.

In the more than 250 years since Johnson penned that, few authors have written anything that will last.

About 350,000 books are published in the United States each year (thank you, Bowker), and of those how many do you suspect stay atop the bedside nightstand or even make it to the nightstand? In percentage terms, books that will be read even a decade after they are first published must be less than a tenth of a percent, and that estimate is probably high. But each one of those books, doomed as the vast majority of them are, has a story behind it and most do (and should) have at least a few "thank-yous" on an acknowledgments page. Nobody does it alone.

Consider movies for a moment. I haven't made or appeared in one of those yet, but I am a promiscuous viewer, indiscriminate in my tastes, except I do not attend horror movies—quite enough of the real stuff going around.

If the movie is good, I'll watch the credits roll, an homage to the many hands that made the picture. If—and, wow, what an if—the film gets to the Oscars and then wins, the director or the producers or the lead actors will stand and mention a few names, perhaps ten.

Regardless of who reads the acknowledgments or stays to watch the credits or hears the speeches, acknowledgments like these are crucial. It's a practice of thanking, a discipline of gratitude that all professions, not just writing and movie mak-ing, could adopt to great effect. If we were all as conscious of the practice of gratitude, we would all be much better off, those who receive the thanks and especially those who give them.

The movie *A Late Quartet* first screened in 2012. I found it fascinating on many levels and discussed it at length on my radio show. The film is about a quartet of classical musicians who have performed together for a quarter of a century when, because of the illness of the cellist, played by Christopher Walken, it is obliged to either change its makeup or break up entirely. The stresses and intimacy of performing for twenty-five years in such a closed universe break out in wonderful performances by Philip Seymour Hoffman, Catherine Keener, and Mark Ivanir alongside Walken, as they come to terms with their own somewhat confused lives and Beethoven's emotional Opus 131.

At one point in the movie, Walken chastises his young students for excessive criticism of each other and relates an anecdote from his early career when the fictional cellist played by Walken met the real genius Pablo Casals. Casals was one of the greatest cellists to have ever lived—he died in 1973—and Walken's character relates two encounters with Casals. The first, when Walken's character was a young student and performed terribly in front of Casals but was praised by him, and then years later when an older Walken had become friends with Casals, and Walken's character chastised the real genius for his insincere praise of the young man's terrible playing years earlier.

Walken then recounts how an angry Casals reached for his cello, struck off the very best parts of the young performer's bad audition from years earlier, and lectured Walken on how he, Casals, chose to concentrate on the good that was there, the uplifting, the hints of talent. Walken then encourages his students to be grateful for the best their colleagues offer, and not to focus on the errors and failings.

It is a wonderful scene in a wonderful movie that did not get much audience at the time, but that will no doubt play forever in the homes of musicians trying to explain what they do and how they live to non-musicians.

The scene I described could well be played for any group involved in any collective effort, for in it is contained a great command on how to live well and happily—by choosing, always choosing, to be grateful for the good that comes one's way rather than to be bitter about disappointments and failures.

A friend credits me with saying to him a long time ago that "we choose to be offended." That casual observation changed how he lived by alerting him to the possibility of choosing *not* to be offended, of waving off so much of the unfortunate stuff of life just as we choose to wave off bad drivers.

The opposite of refusing to be offended is choosing to be grateful. Example: In my twenty-three years of broadcasting and the more than ten thousand interviews I have done, I think I can count on two hands the number of interviewees who have been more than momentarily and dutifully grateful for the opportunity to talk on air about themselves, their projects, or their causes. The vast majority of guests just assume they are great guests and are doing you a favor by showing up. Another set of guests do thank you and really mean it, but they are busy, and even a big interview fades away as a reason for gratitude.

A third group, composed of a very, very few guests, when I meet them again years after our interview, have said to me, "Thank you for that interview you did in _____."

This group is a prompt to me, reminding me to do the same for people who have been kind to me along the way in my media career. Nick Lemann of the *New Yorker*, for example, wrote a wonderful profile of me for his magazine. BookTV's Peter Slen has always been generous in his attention and praise for my books. Mark Steyn, Mark Levin, Fred Barnes, Mark Tapscott, and Sean Hannity have always been great encouragers of my work. The list goes on and on, and I try to recall that and to practice the same sort of generosity of attention and deserved praise when chances come my way.

Two novelists have been exceptionally kind by incorporating a reference to our on-air friendships into their novels; and as both men are extraordinarily gifted writers, these were wonderful surprises.

THE SEVENTH GIFT

Daniel Silva, whose Gabriel Allon novels have taught me so much about Israel and about art history while providing hours of the very best reading available, has invented in his fictional world a unique place, Hewitt Farm, which is owned by the CIA and provides an occasional meeting place for senior servants of the US, Israel, and the UK to gather. The farm is named for a fictional lawyer and lobbyist, and is in the far outskirts of the nation's capital's northern Virginia suburbs. I told Silva on air, in one of our yearly talks about his annual contributions to my education and entertainment, that this was a very wonderful gift indeed, and he told me that such author winks at friends and colleagues are peppered throughout his novels. Now I look for them and, finding them, see a mark of genuine gratitude for friendship of some sort and believe them to be a sign of good humor as well. (Another Hewitt reference appeared in the most recent Silva novel, *The English Girl*, another wink and another example of effortless gratitude to even bit players in large successes.)

C. J. Box is another thriller/mystery writer who makes at least an annual appearance on my program. His Joe Pickett series is terrific stuff. As his books followed the life of a Wyoming game warden through all the woes and intrigues natural to a father of three girls and worker bee in a bureaucracy that deals with some very traditionally lawless regions and people, Chuck introduced Judge Hewitt, "dark and twitchy," along with bailiff Patterson (my senior producer) with walk-on roles. Another couple of winks, another thank-you for the publicity, and a bit of a continuing lift.

Some guests over the years have not only been forgetful of thanks but have been downright hostile. This sort of combativeness is usually the mark of insecurity, pride, or a mixture of both. The presumed entitlement to the floor, as well as a deep distaste for contradiction, make a few folks simply unsuitable for the back-and-forth of a talk show, whether on radio or television.

Thankfully, most of my jousts are with good-humored folks like author and columnist Jonathan Alter, who never fails to express thanks for the shout-out to his books—good, crisp reads about FDR and President Obama—and the chance to speak his piece. Would that all partisans were so committed to the rules of give-and-take. Some have proved remarkably thin skinned; and far from grateful they are still, years later, unhappy with me over some particular clash.

The most famous of my run-ins was with Andrew Sullivan, an old-school, originally British, now American public intellectual of the first rank and a great gift to conversationalists everywhere. We clashed. It was memorable. It did not wound him or me, and we refer to it knowingly as "great radio" when it comes up. Andrew makes me smile. I may make him grind his teeth. No matter. He is a very smart fellow. Long may he ignite.

Several others have sworn off the show in public or private huffs, the opposite of gratitude. Odd, that. But taking offense and hoisting and then nursing a grudge for whatever reason is unlikely to be of use to anyone. No, gratitude in all things, even when cut. If no one in our business cuts you, you aren't worth the time.

Here's a secret: I don't know how one can endure all the sorrows of life without repairing to gratitude. There is such inevitable grief that the practice of gratitude is all that can provide the necessary armor. I wrote the first draft of this chapter on the morning after the night my son relayed to me news of the death of his close friend's brother. I spent some sleepless hours the night before praying for the young man, his brother, and, of course, their parents.

I have been close to a few such catastrophes, beginning with the death of a college roommate, Rick Gottesman, between our junior and senior years. Never have I seen such grief exceeded since Rick's funeral, though sadly I have seen it equaled. How a parent copes is a study I cannot imagine undertaking, but it must have to do with gratitude for the life lived and other blessings, however diminished by the awful, searing loss. Nurturing gratitude is preparation for the worst of days, the building of a compass that will be necessary to get back to life after the deep sorrow abates.

Long ago and far away, when I was a law student at the University of Michigan Law School from 1980 to 1983, I would go to watch the Wolverines play NCAA basketball. The team in those years had a fine point guard by the name of Dan Pelekoudas who later also went to the law school. He became my colleague in a law firm for a few years and a friend who has stayed that way even as our legal careers diverged.

A few years back Dan asked me to read a manuscript written by his best friend about that friend's up-and-down-and-up life. He sent it along. I didn't read it. It sat on the nightstand. For a long time. Dan's wife, Kathy, called Betsy. Would she read it? It was very good. Betsy did. In one day. I still didn't read it, but I did send it to my then-agent, Curtis Yates. Curtis did read it, he loved it, and it quickly became the best-selling *The Color of Rain* by Michael Spehn and Gina Kell Spehn, the best book on grief I have ever read.

The Color of Rain is the story of three wonderful marriages and families, the first two of which saw spouses die of cancer at young ages leaving behind young children and devastated partners. The husband who died and the wife who died had been childhood friends, but their surviving spouses had never met. When they did, they comforted each other through a slow-developing friendship that eventually became love and culminated in marriage. You should read the book as preparation for trials of your own, but it is clear that grieving and gratitude are the only ways to endure the terrible times every life will include.

Practicing gratitude—the careful, daily appreciation, both public and private, of the good people and things in our lives—is a habit. My late pal Coach Jerry would say on almost every occasion of extended conversation, "Life is a habit, Hughie," which meant we fall into patterns both good and bad because that is what we are—pattern-seeking creatures. If we make a habit of gratitude, we will end up giving that habit to most of those around us.

As this is the last of the chapters on the gifts, let me thank those who have made my public career as a writer and a broadcast journalist possible. If this is a bit too autobiographical or tedious, I apologize. I put it here to make skipping over it easy enough. But I wanted to include it because I have so many people to thank for such an extraordinarily fascinating sprint through these fifty-seven years.

I begin with A. T. and Margret Rohl and Hugh and Grace Hewitt. All of them lived in Ashtabula, Ohio. And their respective children Marguerite and William, who produced William, John, and me. The family tree. Who went before those four grand-parents I am not certain, except that James Hewitt set off from Saintfield, Ulster, in 1868, as we have proof in the inscription in his protestant Bible given him at the time of his emigration.

How disappointed his parents would be to know they'd launched a child whose grandson would marry a Catholic lass in far-off Ohio in 1946.

Mrs. Fitting, Sister Mary Columba, Mrs. Was, Sister Mary Benedicte, Ms. Bokone, Mrs. LaRock, Sister Mary Neal, Mr. Santore, Sister Mary Timothy, Sister Mary Aloysius, Mr. Hoover, Mrs. Santucci, and Mr. Karrenbauer: these are the teachers who passed me from Emerson to St. Pius X to St. Mary to Blessed Sacrament to Warren John F. Kennedy High School to Harvard College and Michigan Law School. I won't name the professors who marked me during my time in Cambridge and Ann Arbor for fear of tainting their reputations, but there were many.

David Eisenhower, Richard Nixon, Judges Roger Robb and George MacKinnon, Tex Lazar, William French Smith, Edwin Meese, Fred Fielding, Dick Hauser, John Agresto, Lynne Cheney, and Connie Horner all gave me jobs or kept me in them until I landed in California as a lawyer in private practice in 1989, tending to the Nixon Library with the help of Loie Gaunt, Jack Brennan, Donald Bendetti, and John Taylor.

George Oliva invited me to join the weekend lineup of hosts at KFI radio in Los Angeles in 1990, and Martin Burns did the same for the nightly news and public affairs show at PBS affiliate KCET in 1992. *Life & Times* went on the air in February 1992, and I stayed there as a host alongside Kerman Maddox, Ruebén Martinez, and Patt Morrison until 2002 when the radio show obliged me to take my leave.

Anthony Achoa and Duane Patterson had a hand in bringing me to the attention of Russ Hauth, who in turn urged me on Ed Atsinger, who along with Stu Epperson built Salem Communications. Ed offered me a nationally syndicated radio show in 2000, which Greg Anderson made happen, and which has been nurtured along the way by a dozen senior Salem executives including Tom Tradup. I cannot name every general manager of every station who has been kind to me along the way, but as representatives of that class of long-suffering exec, Brian Taylor and Terry Fahy have served the longest.

My radio show has been remarkably thinly staffed since it began in July 2000, with only Duane Patterson and Adam Ramsey as full-time workers in the radio vineyard; but they have been extraordinary colleagues and wonderful people along the way. More on them later, and on my law partners and faculty colleagues at Chapman Law School, but in passing a shout-out for their generous and inspired help. Danielle Howe Fletcher, who booked guests, graduated from intern to part-time, semi-permanent, always trying to leave but never succeeding: she is a great representative of the nearly fifty interns who have come and gone in my fourteen years of broadcasting.

On the book side, I have partnered with five wonderful publishers and many fine editors, but only two people have attended to every manuscript—Lynne Chapman and Snow Philip. Sheesh, the words they have typed or copyedited respectively.

And finally, to every one of those ten-thousand-plus guests, thank you. Some of them have come again and again through the years, never for money, always for fun, and they get a special thank you: Lileks and Mark Steyn, Emmett of the Unblinking Eye, Erwin Chemerinsky and John Eastman, Fred Barnes and Michael Barone and Bill Kristol, Congressman John Campbell, and the iron man of the show, Congressman David Dreier, who began with us on week one and stayed with us until his time as Chair of Rules was done in December 2012.

Thanks to them all, and to those who will people the next however many years of talking and writing.

What? No mention of family, of the Fetching Mrs. Hewitt and of children? It's a good thing patience isn't one of the seven gifts, but either way the wait is over. Onward.

PART TWO

THE SEVEN GIVERS

THE SPOUSE

Marriage is honorable among all.

—The Epistle to the Hebrews

As I write this, I have been married more than thirty years to the "Fetching Mrs. Hewitt," as I have always referred to her over the air. When our four years of courtship are added in, plus the delay between writing and publication, I will have walked or run the "gift circle" thirty-five times with FMH.

My own dad told me about the gift circle decades ago. Each year, he said, a husband must come through on birthday, anniversary, and Christmas with a winsome gift. There is insurance in numbers, he added. Roll the dice on one present if you will, but don't miss a date and understand you will often miss the mark. Take no offense when a gift is returned.

("Take no offense when a gift is returned" is one of the greatest gifts I ever got from my dad. My wife says that one of the greatest gifts she ever got was from my mom, when my mom told her, as we were about to be married, to never, ever feel obligated to come to their home for any holiday, especially Christmas or Thanksgiving, though we would always be very welcomed. No pressure was there to make an obligatory show up, and no offense taken if for any reason we didn't. That's a wonderful gift, by the way, you parents of sons- and daughters-in-law out there.)

He gave a lot of advice, my dad. Much of it lousy, much of it very good. That is the way with dads, and I suspect my own children will say the same of me. But he was right on the mark when it came to gift giving and wives.

Do the math: I have given gifts to FMH on more than a hundred big occasions. I have trusted in volume—between five and ten items, sometimes more, on Christmases past. I think it fair to guess I have bestowed a thousand presents on my wonderful wife.

As already mentioned, I bat like a Cleveland Indians second baseman, and that may be generous to myself. As I noted at the beginning of this book, I shop mostly at Nordstrom because Nordstrom has an absolutely ironclad return guarantee. No matter what you buy, it can be brought back and returned. And almost everything I have bought FMH has been returned.

Which is fine. It is the gift giving that matters, not the gift keeping. I hope young marrieds know that. I hope especially that young marrieds aren't offended when their beloveds just don't care for their taste in clothing, or anything else. It isn't a rejection of you, or even a commentary on your taste. A returned gift is a reflection of their security in your love, or at least that is what you need to get used to telling yourself if you encourage your spouse to take back what he or she doesn't care for.

It works. That's all I can say. For thirty years it has worked.

As do the bigger gifts, all seven. Spouses need to be their other half's biggest encouragers, support their enthusiasms, jump up with great energy when they rush off to their fray of the day, truly be concerned—empathetic—when they are down or even crushed, laugh at their jokes, thank them for their love often, and graciously put up with their innumerable foibles.

The number one job of the spouse is to care for the other. That is it. Number one. Ahead of children. Ahead of job. Not ahead of God; those two jobs must coexist. But everything else drops to a lower priority. That is how marriage, an improbable and very hard compact, endures—and not merely endures, but flourishes. I have heard people of great faith say that the first job of the spouse is to get their other half to heaven. Okay. Nice summary. But that means getting them through every day, not just to the front of the room on an altar call, though that would be a very good day for a non-believing spouse.

In the Christmas 2012 movie *Parental Guidance* starring Billy Crystal and Bette Midler, Midler explains to their fictional daughter—Crystal and Midler are married in the flick—that Midler cares more for her husband than for her daughter because after she up and left, he stuck around. True, when the spouses do. Sad when they don't.

I won't rehearse the stats on marriage. They are grim and getting grimmer. People don't stick. Because—he said without a lick of training or specialization in the subject, bereft of research or citation—people don't work hard enough at making marriage worth it for their spouse. If you want someone to come home to the same house for decade after decade, then it had better be a happy house, or at least a mostly happy house in which there is a better-than-even chance of being treated better than the concierge at the local hotel would treat them.

I have interviewed thousands of happily married people, and thousands of people who have been divorced. Let me tell you about two couples who made it.

Alan and Marilyn Bergman have been married for fifty-five years as I write this, and are among the most successful songwriter duos ever to collaborate. Together they have been nominated for a dozen Academy Awards and taken home three (for "The Way We Were," "The Windmills of Your Mind," and the score of *Yentl*). Think of the time they must have spent together—far more than the average successful husband and wife, an extraordinary amount of time.

That time was filled with music. Sometimes the obvious needs to be stated.

I interviewed Alan in 2004 after hearing him perform in a small cabaret in Orange County, California, with FMH and our friends Jerry and Susan. His performance and my interview the next day stressed how much Alan and Marilyn laughed together through the long, long years of collaboration. No doubt they had some battles as well, perhaps epic battles. Who doesn't? But of all those gifts, good humor seems to be the one that came easily out of Bergman's many memories when he talked of writing—and living—with his wife.

The second couple is Marsha and Ed Morrissey. Ed was one of the first big bloggers, scribbling away at Captain's Quarters, churning out the prose and politics after his day job as a data manager. Marsha, a wonderfully supportive spouse, didn't scold Ed for wasting his time in front of his computer. She encouraged him; and of all spouses, Marsha should be indulged a touch of selfishness because she is blind. In the course of the decade I have known Ed, she was also the recipient of not one, but two, kidney transplants.

Ed is now a much-admired professional commentator, the captain of HotAir.com; and Marsha remains his extremely supportive wife and partner in many enterprises (happily healthy as well). Both have sought to give everything to each other as needed. An amazing, model marriage is the result.

In fact, in every "model marriage"—and they are all around, marked usually by decades of matrimonial loyalty—both husband and wife are givers, to each other, of numerous and varied gifts. The obvious preconditions of successful gift giving and receiving are there, of course, in the proximity and aligned tastes, knowledge of the other, and even self-interest. As the old and very wise saying goes, "Happy wife, happy life." It can as easily be understood to be said of the wife toward the husband, though not with any easy rhyme. Giving each other the things—practical and impractical, tangible and intangible, expected and unexpected— that are building blocks of happiness is uniquely the opportunity of the married spouse.

In every successful marriage I know there is a similar reciprocity of giving, and not on a small scale but an enormous one. Nothing original here, just a restatement of the obvious. If you want your marriage to thrive and endure decades, give one or more of the seven gifts every day, week, and month. Don't count. Just give. Keep no ledgers. Just give the sorts of gifts that cannot be returned except in the same form to yourself.

I have an entire book to write on marriage, because FMH has made me an expert. She is a gem, a star, a year-round Christmas tree. She is almost always happy unless we are grieving some loss together. She is as unselfish as is possible (not when it comes to shoes), and I look at her sometimes and tell myself the absolute truth: no one else, no one else in the world was better designed for me than she.

Now here is a gooey faith bit, a heads-up for the Hitchens people that you won't like this.

FMH is so perfect for me that I suspect someone along the way was praying specifically that I would be greatly blessed in my marriage. Could have been one of my parents, or both; could have been grandparents or even great-grandparents. My great-grandfather got on a boat in Ulster in 1868, and perhaps his parents whom he would never see again prayed that their lad would be happy and would have children, grandchildren, and great-grandchildren who would marry wonderful husbands and wives. I don't know. I do know I pray that my children will be so blessed and that my grandchildren and great-grandchildren will be so blessed. If you believe in prayer, it makes all the sense in the world to put some markers up on the wall for future generations.

Whatever the source of that prayer, here is my single insight. The God of the universe gave you two jobs: to care for your spouse and to care for your children. You can't do the latter as well as possible without doing the former. That's why it's job number one. And even when divorce intervenes, you have to do your best to forgive and make a modus operandi to keep serving the ex, and thus the kids.

Tough to swallow that, I suppose, but true as true can be. And if you flinch at the thought, and you are still married to spouse one, make today the day you double down on making him or her the center of your life.

It is easier, by the way, with two.

This is one of our phrases, the FMH and I. Whether we are making a bed or driving a long trip, it is always easier with two. That is the gift to see and appreciate. That is the gift that neither of you will want to return.

THE
SECOND
GIVER

THE PARENT

He will turn the hearts of the fathers to the children, and
the hearts of the children to their fathers...

—THE BOOK OF MALACHI

ON THREE WONDERFUL OCCASIONS, THE HAPPIEST DAYS of our lives, Betsy and I became parents to Diana, Will, and James. You have not heard me mention them on air or seen me discuss them in print before this book. Early on, Betsy and I decided that despite our immense love for them and pride in their lives, they would be offstage in a public life. I was afraid that they might become props in a routine, or the objects of scorn or fury that had nothing to do with them.

When they asked me why I never talked about them on air, I explained to them that they really didn't want to deal with the

nuts who sometimes attach themselves to even minor celebri-
ties, and that they didn't want to worry about what their dad said
about them on air. They understood this, and I believe appreciated it more and more as the years went on. Inevitably they got
an occasional, "Oh, you are Hugh Hewitt's daughter [or son]," and
then a reaction conditioned on the speaker's opinion of me. Very
quickly they grasped it as a far better thing to be evaluated on
their own merits and for their own qualities than as an extension
of their parents, especially when one of those parents makes his
living as a pundit.

So I denied the audience the wonderful and often touching
or uproariously funny stories of my children growing up, or how
their experiences formed many of my opinions on all manner of
topics I addressed. I cannot approach the subject of immigration,
for example, without considering what it must mean to a parent
to be separated from a child. I think about military issues from
the perspective of a deployed serviceman or woman separated
from his or her children as I never was for longer than a week.

Public education's successes and its many and obvious failures are for me applications of real-life experiences. All three
of my kids went to wonderful public schools from K through 12,
and two of the three went to great public universities. The truly
attentive listener will be able to figure out which colleges those
were, given my occasional references to them over the past few
years. (My youngest is now finished with college and all have
departed home base. Empty-nester land, here we come.)

I mention this only to assure the reader that what I am about
to write is based on real experience—sixty-three total years of
raising children, adolescents, and young adults, twenty-one
years apiece until each became largely independent.

The seven gifts have specific applications in the context of raising children, but I must underscore the importance of actually showing up to give them. Nothing else compares with quantity when it comes to time spent with children. It is a cliché made of granite-weight truth and diamond hardness. Every minute you are in the house; every minute at their games, plays, concerts; every minute you are at a teacher's conference or sitting next to them laboring over any project is a minute invested. With children, giving the seven gifts starts with giving time.

I could go on and on and on with assertions about the joys and sorrows of parenting, but I don't want to dilute this key core message. The best gift is time with you. Forgo the income, skip the promotion, pass on the party at every possible turn, and be there when they want you to be, even when they don't ask you to.

David Mamet told me that writing a play was like raising a child: the years fly by but the afternoons are endless. Same with every birthday party—seemingly endless. Except now they are long gone and we sit and laugh about them, about bad concerts and awful softball games, interminable swim meets and terrible talent shows, a variety of back-to-school nights, and, of course, slammed doors and arguments about cars and curfews. ("Why can't I drive to Anaheim on New Year's Eve?") There are experts on all these subjects, and Betsy and I are pretty accomplished on some of them, but my take is very, very simple: The biggest gift you can give is yourself. Be profligate.

Here's an astonishing thing about children: they bridge many gulfs if only for a time. In a green room in the Newseum for a broadcast of *This Week with George Stephanopoulos*, the famously ferocious Rahm Emanuel is attending to his twelve-year-old daughter like any other dad in any other room crowded with strangers. None of the flood of famous expletives, just a doting dad.

In the same green room, Arianna Huffington. Now, I have shared dozens of green rooms with Arianna, and have interviewed her scores of times going all the way back to her former husband Michael's unsuccessful Senate run in 1992. A favorite throwaway line of mine when Arianna's name comes up is that I knew Arianna four Ariannas ago. We're like kids in school whose surnames are spelled alike and always get stuck in the same lines together. Arianna and I have passed through two decades of punditry constantly crossing each other's paths. And on every occasion I recall she has daughters, and she recalls I have both sons and a daughter, and we chat about our children's lives. With apparent genuine interest.

Another example. Sean Hannity is a wonderful host to his television guests, charming, welcoming, ready with a laugh. Some in the world of broadcast are remote from their guests, but not Sean, and especially not if you bring along a child, as I did on a couple of occasions. When Sean spots a young man or woman in the green room with their mom or dad, he makes a beeline, sits down, and engages in conversation with them, with the practiced ease of the experienced dad that he is. For Sean, the kid is the most important person in the room.

The dad's club among talk show hosts includes Bill Bennett, Mike Gallagher, Dennis Prager, Michael Medved, and the Great One, Mark Levin. Levin, the combative constitutionalist and extraordinarily gifted polemicist, is a doting and very proud dad, as I am, as we all are.

We serious broadcasters wish for all children that which we wish for our own, and I believe our politics are very much informed by our lives as parents. As I mentioned at the outset of this book, we know the truth of the short statement, "You are only as happy as your least happy child." Even in the throes of harshly contested campaigns, only the lowest of the very low bring children into the fray. I know of no one who does not wish the wonderful Obama daughters all the best that life can offer them and hope that the joy they should have in two loving parents is not diminished by the necessary collisions of American politics.

As I noted before, my first job out of college was working as a research assistant for David Eisenhower in San Clemente, California, on the book that would eventually be titled *Eisenhower at War*, a critically acclaimed survey of his famous grandfather's generalship. But my favorite Eisenhower book isn't the one I worked on. It's David's memoir of his time with his grandfather in Ike and Mamie's retirement at Gettysburg, *Going Home to Glory*. The portrait of Ike as a stern but deeply loving grandfather is not to be missed because, like those television green rooms with children everywhere, it conveys beautifully how absolutely universal are the values of rightly ordered love between parent and child and parent and grandchildren.

Of course there are hundreds of millions of children who do not receive that sort of love, and millions more who have received it only in small portions, served out randomly, the missing guarantee of which adds desperation to a young life.

For more than any other of the givers, this quality of consistent, steady delivery matters. Wives and husbands, friends and coworkers, all can forgive forgetfulness or indulge erratic enthusiasm, or discern patterns when they are hard to see without long experience. But not children. They need and depend upon the steady, intensely personal and parental delivery of the gifts.

In the context of raising future happy adults, the seven gifts have very specific applications. But of all the giver chapters, this one doesn't need much in the way of specific examples. Encouragement, energy, enthusiasm, empathy, good humor, graciousness, and gratitude are self-explanatory in their impact on smalls becoming larges over the course of eighteen to twenty-one years. Of course, parents are also raising their grandchildren as they model how child-rearing will be passed along to the next generation.

The toxic impact on children of the behaviors opposite of the gifts—hypercriticism, lassitude, disinterest, indifference, cruelty, rudeness, and ingratitude—are obvious, and not just in practice, but in the lives of the children living out the reflection of those behaviors. It takes enormous will for a child raised with toxic behaviors who goes on to become a parent to break these embedded patterns. With the assistance of a spouse and teachers, it can be done, but it is hard, very hard. How much easier to have been blessed with parents who were gift givers.

While it is impossible to reclaim time lost, regret over it accomplishes nothing. That is the great message of Dickens's *A Christmas Carol.* An entire life spent in the grip of greed and indifference was not enough to deter the effort of the spirits to reclaim the last few years:

> Scrooge was better than his word. He did it all, and infinitely more; and to Tiny Tim, who did NOT die, he was a second father. He became as good a friend, as good a master, and as good a man, as the good old city knew, or any other good old city, town, or borough, in the good old world.

It is interesting that the book uses Tiny Tim as the hero, along with his father Bob Cratchit, the models of love and gift giving in the midst of poverty. Scrooge, of course, had no children, but after his experience "he was a second father" to Tiny Tim. Reread the description of Scrooge once redeemed: "as good a friend, as good a master, and as good a man, as the good old city knew, or any other good old city, town, or borough, in the good old world." A giver of the gifts, then? Of course.

It wasn't always easy. Read the reaction his change brought among his neighbors:

> Some people laughed to see the alteration in him, but he let them laugh, and little heeded them; for he was wise enough to know that nothing ever happened on this globe for good at which some people did not have their fill of laughter in the outset; and knowing that such as these would be blind anyway, he thought it quite as well that they should wrinkle up their eyes in grins as have the malady in less attractive forms. His own heart laughed: and that was quite enough for him.

Your choice to be a giver of these gifts will trigger exactly this derision among some and especially from the cynical and the "knowing." It is much like demonstrated faith in God, an occasion for mirth among the insecure. People used to defending traditional morals in the public square long ago got used to the guffaws of the elites as those elites celebrate the great change the society is undergoing. Scorn of the many or the few or even one simply does not matter if your "own heart laugh[s]" for the right reasons.

When it comes to the gifts, if your "heart laughs," as did Scrooge's, and if the child smiles, that is enough. And it is proof.

There is nothing to compare with the joy of a happy child become a happy adult, and I suspect that few things could break the heart more than that of a lost or wayward child. Accept and celebrate the blessing of the former and pray hard for the recovery of the latter. That recovery does happen, often, even after incredibly desperate circumstances or deep, deep wounds and harsh words.

An engineering friend of mine recently told me that his son had called him after an unexplained cut-off of more than two years. The son, without explanation, proposed lunch, and my friend, without requesting an explanation, immediately accepted, as, of course, any loving parent would. Who cares why or where they went? They are back. If you have such an estranged child, send them a copy of this book with a Post-it Note attached to this paragraph along with your number. The days are flying by.

An interview I did not get to conduct—though I tried hard to arrange it—was with Henri Nouwen, the Roman Catholic priest and extraordinarily gifted writer. Back when I was making *Searching for God in America*, Martin Burns and I assailed him with requests for a sit-down interview, but got back many patient turndowns. Father Nouwen was exhausted and headed to Europe for a much needed rest, a sabbatical.

He began that sabbatical before we began filming, and he died a year later. His last book, *Sabbatical Journey*, presents the notes from that year.

Perhaps Nouwen's most widely read book is his *The Return of the Prodigal Son: A Story of Homecoming*. It is a long meditation on Rembrandt's painting by the same name, which hangs in the

Hermitage Museum in Saint Petersburg. I have been blessed to see this painting twice on journeys to that city, and I can understand why Nouwen could devote all the days and weeks he did to observing and meditating on it, and writing with such great tenderness about it.

A child estranged from his mother or father should read that book and consider forgiveness for whatever they have done. A parent distanced from a son or daughter should do the same. That gift of forgiveness is not among my numbered gifts because it isn't always and everywhere necessary, but I mention it here as a prompt to what is surely on your mind: What if you did call, write, or e-mail, or reached out through a mutual friend or an old acquaintance? Nothing would be lost by the effort, no pride sacrificed. So what if the party that perpetrated the injury considers that the call is an admission of guilt? So what?

Think of Scrooge and all that time wasted, and think of all the gifts stored up and ready to give.

THE THIRD GIVER

FAMILY MEMBERS

Love one another as I have loved you.

—The Gospel of John

Here's a little exercise. Make a list—right now in the margin—of all first and second family connections. These are your brothers and sisters, your spouse's brothers and sisters, the spouses of all of them, and the children of all of them. The list also includes your parents, your mother-in-law and father-in-law, and all the aunts and uncles on both sides and their children.

This is your family.

Now grade your relationship with each member.

An "A" goes in for genuine friendship, happy-to-see-them joy at the meeting and sadness at the parting.

A "B" is at least occasionally an "A" but with some "C"s and even a "D" thrown in.

A "C" is someone with whom you can watch a football game, do the dishes, go to the movies with, but with whom you could not imagine spending a day or longer alone by choice.

A "D" is a problem, of any sort. "D" is for "dread," as in "I dread seeing Joe or Joan at the big gathering."

"F" means "F"—fail. A catastrophe of a relation. A drunk, or grifter, or bigoted blowhard always smashing up the furniture, if only metaphorically. An ass.

Now, remember how a GPA is arrived at? You get four points for an "A," three for a "B," two for a "C," one for a "D," and zip for an "F." Add up and average your grades and get your family relationship GPA. Here's a secret to happiness: the higher this score, the happier your life, and it has a multiplying effect.

Some of you are looking at big fat zeroes. Toxic families. People in jail. Addicts. Abusers. Controlling, rage-filled in-laws and louts who leer at your sister and tell off-color jokes loudly in restaurants. Steelers fans.

But some, and here I am lucky, score in the high 3s. "Nobody gets the perfect package, Hughie," Coach Jerry was fond of saying. And nobody gets a perfect family.

This short chapter is an appeal to turn the Ds into Cs and the Cs into Bs, while fencing off the fails even at the risk of some hard conversations and a few blowout scenes. Families are hard enough without a malignant propeller guiding every gathering or present in every conversation. Slice 'em out until they change. Help them change if they really and truly want that, but there is no upside in spending years trying to stack sand.

FMH and I are brother and sister to six siblings, five sibling spouses (plus one ex we love and one we simply never see), and nine nephews and nieces. Our parents are gone and most of their generation with them, so it isn't that complicated a matrix. But it is a very, very good one. Blessed and lucky, but also the product of growing to appreciate the gifts of each person in that matrix.

Encouragement of and enthusiasm for the passions of the extended family, empathy for their trials, graciousness and good humor in the face of their oddities and tics, energy when summoned to the tribe's gatherings, and especially gratitude—excessive, absurd, ridiculous amounts of gratitude—for whatever good turns or small blessings they have given you or yours is the ticket, the best ticket, to happiness in the substantial number of days, weeks, months, indeed years, you will be in close contact with your extended family.

Here's a trick I learned early on: this will be the last family gathering before someone among us kicks the bucket. I don't want to be the guy or gal everyone is nodding at during the funeral as the one who ruined Uncle Buck's last family dinner. Sure, it is contrived. But it also works.

Joel the editor pushed me on this chapter, loving the grading system and wanting more.

"What are the gifts that can help us change if we have a lousy relationship with someone in the family?" he queried. "Can we change them? What about political differences? Geographical distance?" Joel is right; there is much to write about these extended family dynamics.

I am not a psychologist, and I didn't stay in a Holiday Inn last night. I was simply lucky in family as I have been abundantly lucky in friends. But there are always rough patches, so about them I can be a little more specific.

In *Mere Christianity*, C. S. Lewis wrote that "[m]en have differed as regards what people you ought to be unselfish to—whether it was only your own family, or your fellow countrymen, or every one. But they have agreed that you ought not to put yourself first." And there is the general rule, the one that will unlock a thousand questions about extended family dynamics: put the other party first, at least insofar as it does not injure your spouse or children.

My mother modeled this early on for Betsy and me, as I noted earlier, taking my new bride aside and telling her to never feel that she had to come to Christmas or Thanksgiving. We went often, but not always, and there wasn't a bit of drama in the decision. Getting rid of the drama and setting aside expectations is the big key to getting along with the in-laws.

Ditto for all family gatherings, large and small. Go if you can, be gracious if you can't. Never ever demand an explanation of someone who must decline your invitation. It is like commenting on food choices and preferences: it just isn't done by the gracious and well mannered. You a vegan? Great! Love fries and cold cuts? Terrific! Don't want to try this new dish? Absolutely fine by me.

Take no offense, even those that are intended. If people leave trash on your front step, you aren't obligated to bring it indoors, nor to return it. And do your best to forgive and forget "episodes," as "episodes" are inevitable. Who doesn't have a family occasion marked by an unexpected fiasco? If you can laugh about that day, great. If not, silence.

Finally, in all of this, keep in mind that the smalls are watching everything, hearing everything, absorbing everything, unconsciously forming the pattern of their own future family interactions. You are building your children's lives far into the future by showing them how to interact with their future extended families. If you wish happiness for them in the future, show them how to manufacture it for others in the present. As you drive away from every gathering, praise those who were there and celebrate what makes them wonderful additions to the family, even if it takes a while and no little inventiveness to come up with an argument. If there is a particularly difficult elder with whom to pass time—and many of us are on the road to being that guy or gal—make a beeline toward them and sit with them at dinner. Demonstrate to your children how to be a peacemaker and a "maker of the feast."

A final note on politics and the extended family. Each year before Thanksgiving I devote a show to the topic of "How to quickly break up the T-Day dinner with a shouting-level argument," and suggest a number of starter lines such as "Sarah Palin would have made a great, great president," or "You know the only thing bad about Obama's terms in office? There can't be three."

The point of the show is to alert everyone to do the opposite: stay away from controversy at family gatherings. There is nothing useful in such conversations. It is a family gathering, not a Fox or MSNBC studio. Post a placard if you have to: *Politics free zone.* Point to it often.

This won't always work, but as with the close of the last chapter on children, so the close of this chapter on family: forgiveness, abundant and even undeserved, may be the biggest gift you can give your extended family, again and again. Or that they can give you. If you hope to receive it, be sure to give it. Often.

FRIENDS

A man who has friends must himself be friendly, but
there is a friend who sticks closer than a brother.

—THE BOOK OF PROVERBS

I FIRST BEGAN WRITING ABOUT FRIENDSHIP FOR MY
senior thesis as an undergraduate when, for some reason now
lost to me, I took on Montaigne's essay on the subject, with asides
on Cicero and Madison.

I liked Montaigne. A professor whose name I have forgotten
offered a course on autobiographies that fit a hole in my fall semes-
ter freshman year, one of those courses that is supposed to happen
to young people attending college. I read Augustine's *Confessions*
and Montaigne's *Essays* and many other fine works that got their
harpoons in me, but none more than the French essayist.

Four years later my tutor, a wonderfully smart fellow by
the name of John Gibbons, suggested adding several different

Roman and American writers on the subject of friendship to my extended scrutiny of Montaigne. That thesis is, woefully, online now with a billion other useless papers. No one warned the Class of 1978 that our college musings would end up instantly accessible by, well, anyone.

I returned to the subject in 1985, in my very first book, *First Principles*, written largely on government time while I didn't do much as an assistant counsel in the Reagan White House. I wasn't lazy, but as I mentioned earlier there was this fellow named Roberts in my suite, and future chief justices tend to shine bright very early and draw the hardest assignments. Plus his memos were funnier than mine.

Friendship matters so much to me because I have been blessed with an extraordinarily good run of great friends. "Lucky in friends" is extraordinarily good luck indeed.

The summer of 2012 found me at the Undertow beach bar in St. Pete's Beach, Florida, with my first friend, John Phillips, who lived down the way from me on Arthur Street until we hit age seven and moved to Warren's east side where we still lived less than a mile apart. Joining us at the Undertow was our mutual high school pal Phil Mokris, with whom I shared many rounds of golf (penance for him) and beery nights from high school forward.*

---

*As this is a memoir of sorts, let the record show that, in the company of the aforementioned Philip Mokris, and while a duly enrolled member of the John F. Kennedy High School Golf Team of 1974, I recorded a 39. When my disbelieving son, Will, in a display of churlish and deeply disrespectful skepticism, questioned this accomplishment, I texted Mokris for confirmation. He responded, "Will, for reasons I cannot explain, your father did shoot 39 in a match which I witnessed and coached him. I shot 38 and was so excited for him I had to make a three footer on the last hole so he wouldn't be ragging on me now. Unfortunately for your dad it was next year we won state after we got the riffraff off our squad." This text exchange is evidence of a deep friendship. I smile as I reread it in the editing phase. It will make me smile forever, for it was a wonderful day, but one that evolved into a wonderful three-way exchange with my son.

My Ohio youth was spent largely in the company of these two and a gang of others that included Phil's brother Paul, Kim and Scott Phillips, Greg Reynolds, Mark Peterson, Steven Pisanelli, and an equivalent number of girls—Pattie Guarnieri, Mary Pat Wilson, Molly McGuire, Jacquie Stanislaw. I name them not to inform on them or educate the reader but to please myself. Memories of them make me smile as they themselves do when I see or talk with them. A youth rich with good friends is the best guarantee of at least intermittent happiness throughout however long a life you lead.

The friend with whom I spent the most time, talked the longest, traveled the farthest, was, is, and I hope remains for many years more, Rob Guarnieri, who has been my "particular friend" (as Royal Navy captain Jack Aubrey of *Master and Commander* fame would say of surgeon and spy Stephen Maturin) since the playground of Blessed Sacrament School in the late sixties.

I do not have the pages to describe our adventures or our laughs, but they are immense and continuing. Just recently, Guarnieri invited me to partner with him through a forty-five hole "best ball" golf extravaganza, during which I contributed two holes. The golfers will instantly recognize how great a level of futility this represents, but Rob did not complain (though he did repeatedly offer me 5-hour Energy shots in a touching display of optimism in the face of incontrovertible facts, facts he had been dealing with since at least 1969). Two months ago I attended the wedding of his son Bret—my godson—and every time I see Rob, whether for high ceremony or low, low sport, it is simply another page in a very long and very good book of friendship.

Male friendship requires an enormous amount of time and very little conversation, though the latter can and often does occur and reaches great depth of emotion and meaning. But those conversations are separated by hundreds, if not thousands, of hours of amiable, pleasant chatter, mostly about sports, women generally, girlfriends and wives particularly, children, and business. I do not presume to judge friendship between women, but there is a joy in hours and hours of companionship void of any deep conversation. Guarnieri and I have spent more time talking about the Cleveland Indians, Browns, and Cavs than anything of consequence, and it is those hours that have allowed our friendship to grow so deep. My natural brothers, Bill and John, are good friends and much loved, and we spend hours of conversation on the same topics, but I know for a fact I have spent more hours talking with Rob than with any other person on the planet who is not my wife or child. A particular friend indeed.

When I headed to college, I was lucky again in friends, with a group that extended across classes and genders, politics and faiths. Mark Gearan, Dan Poneman, and Paul Mulkerin were first among equals, and Regina Pisa was our fifth on most adventures as well as long and boring afternoons in the Winthrop House library. These three are all Democrats, by the way, and it is my experience that fierce partisans are more often than not found in great friendships that cross all aisles.

Mark Gearan was well known to almost every Democrat of rank during the Clinton years, as he was the forty-second president's deputy chief of staff, director of communications, and then head of the Peace Corps. We watched the famed *60 Minutes* interview together in 1992 during one of my occasional visits back to DC, me shaking my head in near disgust, and Mark thrilled with the performance of the Comeback Kid and the future secretary of state.

I have not had a chance to ask many interviewees about their closest friends, or about opposites loving the company of each other, but I know from the campaign of 2008 that the friendship of Joe Lieberman and John McCain was so profound that the former underwent enormous scorn and vituperation from the left to work the campaign trail for the GOP nominee.

I shared a Cleveland stage with the Connecticut senator during the campaign, along with my radio pals Dennis Prager and Michael Medved. Lieberman's heartfelt appeal for his friend was touching, the product not so much of their shared understanding of the threat that America faced (and faces) from radical Islam, but of decades of side-by-side work in the Senate. There have been many such friendships, but none so obviously elevated above partisanship as when a former national nominee of one party campaigned for the national nominee of the other. Rare, and worth asking yourself if there is anyone like that in your life, willing to endure that kind of savage criticism for the sake of your friendship.

When I left DC for California, I was blessed to quickly meet and be befriended by two extraordinary men. Bill Lobdell is, but for his birth outside of Youngstown, Ohio, not far from my hometown of Warren, a lifelong Californian; and except for a few of his most recent adult years, a lifelong journalist as well, with most of that time spent at the *Los Angeles Times,* the outlet I had the most scorn for until its irrelevance rendered it not worth the time that scorn requires. Mark D. Roberts is one of the best theologians of our age and was, for a long season, a great pastor in California before his calling took him to Texas.

Bill and Mark became very close friends of mine and, as often happened in my broadcast career, regular guests on my radio show: Bill because he would try and defend the *Times* on this or that subject, Mark on the various theological issues of the day.

It is great fun to interview your close friends, but perilous as well because inside jokes or knowing asides are lost on audience members tuning in for a brief sampling or especially a first listen. Increasingly, cable sets are full of such back-and-forths, entertaining to the participants but not to the audience. Too much of media is already a closed universe for elites, and the further narrowing of the content to inside baseball between pals is a recipe for ratings failure. The radio, though, is more forgiving of some such chatter than television, and Lobdell and Roberts shared part of my life that made our friendships unique. That is part of the joy of friendship—experiencing a second life, if only for a short time.

Some friendships fade. Others dissolve under stress or disagreement. Still other friends just leave. Those that stick, however, are almost irreplaceable; and the sadness of long life is losing friends. In 2012 I attended funerals for my friend and longtime dentist Jerry Kushner, my friend and longtime political ally Tom Fuentes, and my friend and next-door neighbor Jerry Tardie. When the decade opened I expected each of them to be fixtures of each of its years, and my companions over many, many dinners. I had known Tom since 1978, Jerry and Jerry since 1990.

The deaths of such close friends confirmed for me the downside of friendship but also its greatest gift, which is that of encouragement. Thinking about what I had lost in that long year, I found that it was the cheerful—often teasingly so—encouragement of my friends to keep on doing whatever it was I enjoyed doing, whether it was politics, sports, or movies. This is what the best of friends do: encourage their friends to live life fully and with joy, unapologetically taking the best things in life, whether faith, family, or passions, and following them all. I cannot name them all—the Buds, Mikes, Garys, Emmetts, or Tims—or describe how even an occasional meeting with a Dennis or an Andrew, a John or a Geoff, a Cliff, a Larry, or a Twiggs can add sparkle and lift to a week or a month, but the reality of the preciousness of friendship is something I have tried hard to pass on to my children, urging them to take care that their friends are kept close and their needs as far as possible met.

Some friends are those of the office only or mostly. For me, Duane and Adam and Anthony are four-hour-a-day intimates, pals, and professional colleagues for whom I would do much and who have done much for me. Some people hate going to work. I love heading to my studio, even when Sinister Del is there (Duane's dad and a wonderful volunteer retiree set of hands). Such workplaces are rare, but you can work to create them, slowly, over time.

Some friendships will fade because of distance or end because of irreconcilable disagreement, but losing a friend is like a chapter torn from a book. Try to replace it, even if the trying has to be postponed again and again and the trying extends over many years. As I write that line I think of two friends lost to me by deep disagreement, each the source more of sorrow than anger now, but also probably beyond repair in this life. That's life in a fallen world. Both were casualties of trying to be in business with a friend. When it works—and it has for me, often—it is wonderful. But what a risk. Be aware of it.

I suppose some of you who have read this far will be clueless as to what I am writing about, and I can't really recommend you go and find a friend. It isn't at all like joining a bowling league or subscribing to a new magazine. You either have friends or you don't, and lacking them late in life is a real obstacle to enjoying life as our options narrow with the years. But to the extent you have them, or can renew them, take those friendships and hold them close and sprinkle the encouragement on with abandon.

"There is nothing better than a trusted friend," said Euripides, "neither wealth nor princely power; mere number is a senseless thing to set off against a noble friend."

This bit of wisdom, says Thomas Jefferson biographer Jon Meacham, was one of the entries in the third president's "literary commonplace book in which he copied passages that struck him as important."[1] Jefferson never lacked for great friends, though his closest friend of childhood and his early years, Dabney Carr, died before he was thirty after marrying Jefferson's sister. "His grief seemed to surpass that of his reaction to his sister Jane's death," said Meacham in his book *Thomas Jefferson: The Art of Power.*

The loss of his closest friend did not stop Jefferson from giving himself again and again in great friendships with like-minded men, and sometimes with men who agreed only occasionally and sometimes with men of completely opposite temperaments and opinions, such as John Adams. If, as many believe, Jefferson was the most accomplished American—not the greatest, but the most accomplished—part of that set of achievements has to be his capacity for friendship.

Friendship is much like the love that is described in Paul's first epistle to the Corinthians: "Love is patient, love is kind. It does not envy, it does not boast, it is not proud. It does not dishonor others, it is not self-seeking, it is not easily angered, it keeps no record of wrongs. Love does not delight in evil but rejoices with the truth. It always protects, always trusts, always hopes, always perseveres. Love never fails" (13:4–8 NIV).

THE FIFTH GIVER

THE COWORKER

Two are better than one, because they have a good return
for their labor: If either of them falls down, one can help
the other up.

—THE BOOK OF ECCLESIASTES (NIV)

BY AGE FIFTY-SEVEN, I HAVE WORKED IN THE FOLLOWING
places: Warren, Ohio's Packard Park City Pool and the White
House; Richard Nixon's Casa Pacifica and four law firms, includ-
ing Gibson, Dunn and Crutcher offices in LA, DC, and Newport
Beach, California; the United States Court of Appeals for the
District of Columbia Circuit and the Los Angeles radio station
KFI on the weekend night shift; PBS and the Richard Nixon
Library; radio stations across the country via syndication, with
GMs and program directors and sales staff in each and every one

of the one hundred–plus affiliates that have carried my show; the US attorney general's fifth-floor suite in the Department of Justice; the National Endowment for the Humanities, the United States Office of Personnel Management, and a half dozen publishing houses, four magazines, and a newspaper, as well as countless freelance assignments and hundreds of speaking gigs.

I have had more jobs than I can actually remember. My first was as a caddy, which I did for years. I can't golf worth a lick, but I could carry back-to-back doubles back in the day. I did an entire three-hour radio show on the lessons learned from caddying. First lesson: people cheat. Important one to learn, that.

I have jobs for which I am not paid or am paid only a token. I am on my Presbyterian church's session and have been for four years. Lots of hours there. Thank goodness my Catholic church doesn't want my time.

I have served for fifteen years on the Orange County Children and Families Commission, one of nine members who give tax dollars to programs helping children five and under achieve school readiness by increasing their health and learning capability. Great fun, and meaningful beyond words. It is perhaps the single most effective government agency I have ever been involved with. Most of my colleagues there are doctors and health and education professionals—amazing people whom most lawyers and journalists never get to really work with.

Before the commission, I served a half dozen years on the California Arts Council. My friends with genuine knowledge of the arts cringe at this; they know I am relentlessly middlebrow, deaf to fine music, and blind to much that is beautiful. But the middlebrow deserve a voice. Keep in mind the famous assessment of Supreme Court nominee Harrold Carswell, by Senator

Roman Hruska. "Even if he were mediocre, there are a lot of mediocre judges and people and lawyers," he said. "They are entitled to a little representation, aren't they, and a little chance? We can't have all Brandeises, Frankfurters and Cardozos." And on the Arts Council, we can't all be Pollocks or Pearlmans. But hanging with the arts crowd for a half dozen years through our monthly meetings was a blast and a different group altogether.

The one appointment I had for which I was genuinely qualified, perhaps better than anyone else in California, was as a board member of the South Coast Air Quality Management District, a vastly powerful environmental agency to which former California governor Pete Wilson nominated me in 1990 and on which I served for a year until Democrats in the state's senate threw me off. Having served as general counsel for two federal agencies, and the deputy director of the much larger United States Office of Personnel Management under President Reagan, I had gone through United States Senate confirmation.*

Having carried some of the highest security clearances in the country, even the ominously named SCI, code name VEIL (see Woodward's book by that title), I had been the subject of four FBI full-field background clearances and am relentlessly squeaky clean. So I knew the law, knew government, was fully vetted—and was still tossed off by the Democrats because I knew the area and opposed stupid, as compared to effective, regulation. This is government. But I digress. At the South Coast AQMD, my usual group of colleagues were scientists of the first order.

I am a member of the faculty of Chapman University School of Law and have been since we opened the doors in 1995, and thus

---

* Given unanimously, I'll add. Thank you, Senators Kennedy, Kerry, and Byrd, among other wildly lefty Democrats voting at the time.

a colleague of scores of incredibly talented scholars and teachers, as well as of hundreds of absolutely first-rate staff and students. I am a partner in my third law firm, and have had—and still have— terrific law partners of the highest rank and ability. I love even my litigator colleagues, a joke other lawyers will get. Litigators have what are called "high motors" in the NBA, and the best—and I work with the best defense counsel in the land, the folks who get called when the trial is going to go and the stakes are very high— have motors set on high, high speed all the time. Tiring, but not wearisome, wonderful if challenging, the very best sort of professionals in a profession often mocked until someone needs help, and then a lifeline.

My broadcast career has included stints at one huge radio station—Los Angeles KFI—one great television station—LA's KCET—and two great networks, PBS and Salem Communications. My on-air colleagues include the estimable writer/reporter Patt Morrison; one of the very best people on the side of the Democrats, Kerman Maddox; and the very best set of national and local talk show hosts anywhere, which includes Bill Bennett, Mike Gallagher, Dennis Prager, and Michael Medved, plus a team of behind-the-scenes communications professionals defined as much by their deep faith lives and commitment to the good as by success, which has been immense.

I have asked one of Salem's two founders, Ed Atsinger, to join me on air to discuss his and his brother-in-law Stu Epperson's remarkable achievement, but his modesty, as real as his immense success, led him to decline. Enough to say that Harvard Business School ought to make a study of this company if it wants to know how to make, keep, and grow a genuine culture of excellence committed to the highest purposes. Part of that culture is to hire and keep people as Salem has, like Russ Hauth and Greg Anderson and Terry Fahy, not for years but for decades. Part of that culture is to recruit, recruit, recruit for excellence, so that the Russell Shubins, David Spadys, Greg Hengles, and Derek Fowlers of the world populate every office on every floor.

In all those settings I had colleagues. Ten at the Arts Council. Eight on the Children's Commission. Eight on the AQMD. Part-time colleagues, but colleagues. Scores of colleagues on the faculty, dozens of law partners over the years, hundreds of fellow workers in the vineyards at Salem and before that at KCET and KFI. (My very first call screener, on my very first day of radio, was Marc Germain, himself destined to be a hugely successful on-air personality and a dear friend. God has always blessed me with remarkable people at the strangest places. Chrystal was my first secretary—ever—and kept a young DOJ lawyer from making ridiculous mistakes. Both Marc and Chrystal were work colleagues for only a very short time, but crucial to my life. There are people like that in yours as well, to whom the gift of gratitude is owed as I owe them.)

The world's very best lawyers have been my colleagues (I can say that with complete confidence: the Chief Justice counts because of our time together in the White House Counsel's office, led by the remarkable Fred Fielding and co-captained by Dick Hauser, two of the most professional "wise counselors" any president could ever hope for). I count one of my current partners, Gary Wolensky, as among the best trial lawyers on product liability defense in the land, and have often had John Eastman, one of the best appellate advocates around, as a colleague on cases. The two attorneys general I served, William French

Smith and Edwin Meese, were great leaders of the world's most renowned justice department, a model and beacon for the rule of law. I know lawyers.

I have worked both for and with strong, strong women. Lynne Cheney was my boss for a brief time at the National Endowment for the Humanities, a forceful but cheerful leader whom the country would get to know through her terrific service for eight years, mostly of war, and from many "undisclosed locations" at the side of Vice President Dick Cheney. (Every Cheney adult—the Veep and Mrs., Liz and Mary, have been terrific guests on the radio show, and may represent the only full family set of interviews I have done. Wonderful guests, each of them, and a remarkable family of public servants. After the election of 2004, the Cheneys hosted a few pundits at the Naval Observatory for a dinner that looked back as well as forward. What I recall the most was the easy amiability and genuine candor of the vice president who, like his friend Donald Rumsfeld, held public service so great a virtue that they would endure without complaint the vilification of the citizens they served so selflessly, and do so with amazing good humor.)

I went from being Lynne Cheney's general counsel to being Connie Horner's top lawyer at the United States Office of Personnel Management, another strong woman with great good humor, and today am law partners with two extraordinarily talented women, Janet Hickson and Liz McNulty, who combine being great moms with being the best advocates any client could want. (Liz is going to be famous as one of the few lawyers in the country who understand the nightmare of California's "green chemistry" regs as well as its uniquely stupid and costly Proposition 65 rules. How she manages these crazy regulatory regimes pales in comparison to the supervision of her five children under ten, which she shares with husband Bart. There's a book there, but only a high-powered lawyer-mom can write it.) I know powerful women.

One of the world's most significant political figures of the post–World War II era was my boss for nearly two years beginning in 1978 and then again for another two years in 1989 when I oversaw the construction and opening of his presidential library in Yorba Linda, California. Richard Nixon was an extraordinary man, and hundreds of conversations with President Nixon in his retirement gave me a window into the world of the very powerful, beginning when I was twenty-two. Working closely with Nixon from a relatively early age took all the awe out of me for men and women of high office, though not admiration or respect. The early immersion in the life of a once powerful—the once most powerful, in fact—man prepared me to study with clarity the conduct of other powerful men.

I can't count the governors, senators, congressmen, and other officials who have crossed my path on air and off. I know pols. Love them too; they are for the most part honorable and hardworking men and women of high purpose even if they are ambitious. Ambition is fine. "Fame is the highest ambition of the noblest minds," said Alexander Hamilton. There have been some rotters, some genuinely bad guys who ended up down the hall or across the way, but very few. Most, like Nixon, had tremendous gifts and some flaws, just like me and just like you. The higher the position, the greater the opportunity to succeed and fail.

I have worked and/or interviewed with the very best journalists on the planet. I have been interviewed by Charlie Rose, the best news interviewer on the planet, and by his successor-in-interest, Jake Tapper. I have interviewed, as mentioned earlier, the best broadcaster on the planet, Vin Scully. I have spent hours and hours and hours, on air and off, with some of the most influential preachers of our age—Rick Warren, Chuck Colson, Greg Laurie, to name just three who have preached to millions and millions. Journalists and preachers are very similar personalities, though the latter readily admit to wanting to persuade their audiences of particular messages, and most of the former resist that description.

And add to this list of professional colleagues other unique sets of professionals I have had the pleasure of working with:

Scientists of the very first rank. The very best doctors in the world on conditions like autism, childhood obesity, and asthma. Performers and artists of the very first rank. Singers, songwriters, and dancers. Authors of every conceivable variety. And service workers by the hundreds. Drivers of cars and secretaries, too many to recall. Cleaning crews and gardeners. Add in academics and cynical political consultants and the radio and television people, from stage managers to sound engineers.[*]

And, of course, I think I have interviewed people holding every conceivable kind of job. They are all interesting. Even the ethnomusicologist who was enraged that I referred to women as "gals" and who thought the playing of loud music directed to terrorists was torture.

I have even had the great pleasure of working alongside

---

[*] My pal and my technical genius on all matters electronic, Anthony Ochoa, may be the best radio engineer in the world but, like most radio engineers, his passion for perfection has taught me that perfectionists make for very interesting wrestling colleagues! We love Anthony and depend upon him, but after a twenty-four-hour remote setup, well, he's a colleague with an attitude!

extraordinary philanthropists whose job it is to do good, and college presidents whose job it is to teach the next generation to do good.

Foster Friess is a wonderfully generous man who is always giving, and he and his wife, Lynne, dropped by the studio for a visit and a hamburger and you would never know one of the country's great philanthropists was sitting in Ruby's. Jack and Pina Templeton are good friends who have traveled with Betsy and me to funny, far-off places, and are always alert to the needs of others. Both Templetons are accomplished medical doctors as well as captains of vast foundations that pioneer important work at the intersection of faith and reason, and both are as modest as the most modest person you know.

I count four college presidents as colleagues, including Chapman University's remarkable Jim Doti who has done more with one college in one span of years than any other college president I know of.

Given more years, Bill Armstrong, the former United States senator from Colorado, and President Corey of Biola University might catch Jim, and both are building lighthouse institutions from the great foundations they inherited.

Dr. Larry Arnn, president of Hillsdale College, is more than a colleague and even more than a great and good friend. He is my teacher of teachers, and if you have any chance to spend a day with him, you should, though if you are a person of means, you will end up leaving some of your fortune with him to do the work of Hillsdale, which is nothing less than the work of renewing the Republic.

There is a key takeaway from having held all these jobs, had all these sorts of colleagues, and interviewed all these sorts of people: I owed each one of them something, though I am not sure how often I gave it to them. The purpose of this catalogue is to provoke in you an ordering of your own, the long list of people who, whether you knew it then or not, helped you become your professional self, and because your professional self—your working self—is part and parcel of who you are and how you will stand before God as a completed life, each of them figures in all that you have done or created that is good, including your marriage and your children, and every one of the good things you count as your good works. They are all community property, and all these colleagues of mine, just like all those colleagues of yours, are co-owners.

All these jobs, positions, and people changed my life as I did theirs, every single day I went to work. Every day in every job in the world, we are being influenced and are influencing the people with whom we work. Lawyers and officials, bosses and colleagues, men and women, journalists and guests, preachers and teachers—all these people are a kaleidoscope of connections that has its counterpart in every single life, even if the names attached to the flow chart of jobs and coworkers doesn't have the same level of instant recognition as, say, the name Nixon does. What matters is the volume of people with whom we work over the course of our lives. One teacher, for example, in a moderately sized high school probably has more colleagues over the course of a career than I have had. Most people have dozens and dozens of coworkers, though the passing parade is sometimes not noticed for its familiarity.

To a degree that is almost impossible to understand, the interconnectedness of the lives of those who work together permeates our whole being. We just don't pause to think about it much because, like the air we breathe, we take for granted that we are actually working with other human beings.

I have used six non-scriptural quotes more than any others. Three are from my dozen-plus years behind the microphone on my syndicated radio show:

1. "Morning glory and evening grace."
2. "If only I had a producer."
3. "Not going to do it. Wouldn't be prudent." (In homage to the first President Bush.)

The other three quotes have served me in my twin interests of politics and faith. On all things political I remind myself of Benjamin Disraeli's admonition: "A majority is better than the best repartee." That sums up all politics.

And with regards to faith—and especially with regards to the hundreds of thousands of people whose lives I have at least briefly touched well or poorly through my work (and believe it or not, the thousands every reader of this book, including you, have at a minimum touched)—C. S. Lewis's warning from his essay "The Weight of Glory," which I touched in the chapter on graciousness:

There are no *ordinary* people. You have never talked to a mere mortal. Nations, cultures, arts, civilizations—these are mortal, and their life is to ours as the life of a gnat. But it is immortals whom we joke with, work with, marry, snub, and exploit—immortal horrors or everlasting splendours. This does not mean that we are to be perpetually solemn. We must play. But our merriment must be of that kind (and it is, in fact, the merriest kind) which exists between people who have, from the outset, taken each other seriously—no flippancy, no superiority, no presumption. And our charity must be a real and costly love, with deep feeling for the sins in spite of which we love the sinner—no mere tolerance, or indulgence which parodies love as flippancy parodies merriment. Next to the Blessed Sacrament itself, your neighbor is the holiest object presented to your senses. If he is your Christian neighbour, he is holy in almost the same way, for in him also Christ *vere latitat*, the glorifier and the glorified, Glory Himself, is truly hidden.

Every single one of the people you have worked with, for however brief a period of time and no matter what their position, was an eternal soul on the brink of eternal glory or its opposite. All those interactions, every single one of those hellos, good-byes, and everything in between has to be understood in light of Lewis's observation, and this second Lewis insight as well—quote number six—from his essay "Christianity and Culture": "There is no neutral ground in the universe: every square inch, every split second, is claimed by God and counter-claimed by Satan."

This is the perspective that Christians need to bring to work, all their work, all their "jobs," volunteer or paid, and all the people there. Every gift is owed to every single person you encounter. An impossible amount of giving, I know, but we ought to be exhausted in the attempt, not benignly ignorant of the occasion as I so often am.

How often, I have to wonder, have I absolutely failed to see the need I could have met from a colleague, if only for an encouraging word or a bit of good humor shared, or empathy with pain being suffered? The logbook of my missed opportunities is very thick. I am confident of forgiveness but regretful that this basic disposition, of which I have been aware of the duty to adopt for decades, is still a daily challenge.

The three people with whom I have worked most closely for the longest period of time are Lynne, Duane, and Adam. Lynne has been my assistant since 1989, Duane my senior producer, and Adam my engineer since July 2000. They are amazing people, and their stories of achievement and overcoming adversity are inspiring, each in its own way. I hope I have served them as they have served me, but we cannot know until God provides the perfect and complete accounting at our judging.

As I mentioned earlier, my friend David Allen White loves to quote the old Catholic command to think on four things every day: death, judgment, heaven, and hell. Not cheery, but wise. In that process, add this layer of thought: Witnesses at that judgment will include everyone—everyone—with whom you have ever worked. Their testimony will be complete.

There is one passage in literature that, better than any other I have known, captures the idea of the responsibility of working, both within the workplace and how we use the fruits of our work. It is another nugget from Dickens's *A Christmas Carol*. It is Scrooge's interview with the ghost of his business partner, Marley, who has returned to warn Scrooge about the course he is on. Marley rebukes Scrooge, but only with complete knowledge of how he, the ghost, had utterly failed to comprehend his real work while alive:

> "Know that any Christian spirit working kindly in its little sphere, whatever it may be, will find its mortal life too short for its vast means of usefulness.... Yet such was I!...

"Mankind was my business. The common welfare was my business; charity, mercy, forbearance, and benevolence, were all my business. The dealings of my trade were but a drop of water in the comprehensive ocean of my business!"

Marley wears a chain forged of his neglect of his duties beyond his official work, his lack of being useful to others to whom he might have been useful. He warns Scrooge about the one he was busy making for himself. As if to magnify the alarm, Scrooge catches a glimpse of others in the same self-made trap as Marley:

The air was filled with phantoms, wandering hither and thither in restless haste, and moaning as they went. Every one of them wore chains like Marley's Ghost; some few (they might be guilty governments) were linked together; none were free. Many had been personally known to Scrooge in their lives. He had been quite familiar with one old ghost, in a white waist-coat, with a monstrous iron safe attached to its ankle, who cried piteously at being unable to assist a wretched woman with an infant, whom it saw below, upon a doorstep. The misery with them all was, clearly, that they sought to interfere, for good, in human matters, and had lost the power for ever.

The time to offer the gifts is now. No one can bank on tomorrow or the far distant retirement as a time of being useful to others.

"Action this day!" Winston Churchill would scribble on wartime memo after memo. That is an admonition we can all use when considering our coworkers, all they need, and all we can provide.

THE SIXTH GIVER

TEACHERS

Incline your ear and hear the words of the wise, and apply your heart to my knowledge...

—THE BOOK OF PROVERBS

As I mentioned in an earlier chapter, in two decades of interviews for both television and radio, only once did I run out of tape. My guests often put limits on the length of time they were available for questions. Then there are the limits imposed by the radio and television formats. But then...

I sat down with actor Richard Dreyfuss. It was a two-camera shoot for the PBS Los Angeles show I cohosted from 1992 to 2002, *Life and Times*. Often we would drag the cameras out to do a sit-down with a Hollywood type who felt like going high-end for a public television sit-down. Thus I chatted away with Oliver Stone and Sidney Kramer, Anthony Minghella and Donald Sutherland, Charlton Heston and Tracey Ulhman. And a score of others, including Dreyfuss. These interviews always required a lot of work for me, as I am not a student of Hollywood, just a lover of movies. Thus I had to rewatch a few films and read all the interviews I could get my hands on.

I don't have a transcript of the thirty-minute conversation with Dreyfuss as it was edited into final form and aired, and is now buried in the KCET vault. But at some point in the three hours that did make it into the final cut, I asked Dreyfuss if he was happy with his career and his choices. The man who made *Mr. Holland's Opus* unexpectedly said he would trade it all to have been a high school history teacher in Indiana.

I think he said Indiana. Memory is a funny thing. Perhaps he said Illinois. Either way, I didn't believe him at the time. Neither did a great number of our viewers who wrote in (this was before e-mail) or phoned the call-in comment line with skepticism in their voices. Many in the audience couldn't believe that anyone would exchange the fame and fortune of a Hollywood star for the life of a teacher.

Teachers don't make much money. They work very hard, deal with incredible frustrations, and often suffer ten horrible students for every good one. Parents are often either nightmares demanding special treatment or absent entirely. Principals can be terrible, and classrooms crowded with old books and lousy heating or ventilation. Some students threaten physical mayhem. Others are needy beyond words. Rarely does recognition follow talent and effort; thanks are equally rare.

Still, the country has about 3.7 million elementary and secondary public and private school teachers. Think on that number for a bit. What a huge profession. What a huge calling. Who answers that call? Who is attracted to a relatively low-paying profession with long hours and little thanks and recognition? Why would Richard Dreyfuss even muse about exchanging an Oscar and tens of millions in salary for such a job?

An occasional guest of mine from over the years has been *Washington Post* scribe Jay Mathews. Jay has been writing about education for years, and his book *Work Hard. Be Nice.* was the subject of one of my rare three-hour interviews when it first appeared in 2009.

I mentioned this book earlier, but now for the underlining. *Work Hard. Be Nice.* is the story of the Knowledge Is Power Program, or "KIPP," which is slowly changing the face of urban public education in America.

Note that there are many other great school choice systems. I am on the board of one such extraordinary effort, the Great Hearts Academies system, begun in Arizona and now exporting its wildly successful model to Texas and other states. A thousand flowers are blooming in public education—well, at least hundreds—and they all need champions. KIPP, though, got the ball rolling in my field of vision, so I'll spend some time on it here.

The inner city has always had its share of enormously gifted and dedicated teachers, and occasionally one of their stories will escape into the public eye, and he or she will be celebrated. Think Jaime Escalante, the real-life hero of *Stand and Deliver*. But it is tough, hard work; and as the test scores will tell anyone who reads them, we have been losing a battle to educate underclass kids, a battle that America used to win routinely.

Mathews introduces us to Michael Feinberg and Dave Levin, two Ivy league graduates who signed up for Teach for America in

1990, failed miserably in their first months in the classroom, and then began a program of bringing their desperately poor students to discipline and enthusiasm, long school days, Saturday and summer school, and rewards based on achievement. Nearly two decades later, the KIPP charter school effort they began in Houston and the Bronx has spread to sixty-six schools in nineteen states enrolling fourteen thousand students. It continues to grow thanks to the crucial support of Gap founders Doris and Don Fisher, their talent scouts Scott Hamilton and Stacey Boyd, and enthusiastic school superintendents across the country, recruiting new teachers, students, and parents, and opening new schools in welcoming districts. With every new success, KIPP proves again that many hundreds of thousands of kids who are warehoused in failing schools are perfectly capable of achieving in middle school, succeeding in high school, and graduating from college.

There are no secrets in KIPP—just old lessons relearned and embraced by committed teachers willing to bring astonishing levels of energy to their classrooms. The charter school movement has always had its enemies, and KIPP has its share of critics. Their opinions are fairly chronicled by Mathews. But this veteran of almost thirty years of excellent reporting on schools cannot help leaving readers amazed and impressed by what KIPP has accomplished and the charisma of its founders and associated heroes. It's clear there is no good reason why millions of American children have to emerge from middle schools unprepared for high school and the life beyond it. The drama of turning around schools is the drama of turning around lives. It is why *Goodbye, Mr. Chips, To Sir with Love, Stand and Deliver*, and, yes, *Mr. Holland's Opus* are movies with followings that never die off.

After Jay wrote the book and came on the show, I joined the board of Great Hearts Academies of Arizona as noted above, a public charter school system in the Grand Canyon state that is rapidly growing and changing the way things are done in Arizona schools. The waiting list is long for these classically organized schools. They are hard to get into and difficult to succeed in, but they prepare students.

And they attract great teachers, many of them from Hillsdale College and other colleges dedicated to classical, liberal arts education such as Thomas Aquinas College. Great colleges produce great, dedicated teachers. Great Hearts doesn't offer the same set of benefits that other public schools in Arizona do, but new teachers flock to them because of the purpose they serve, the order they observe, and the results they achieve. These teachers and those like them across America are gift givers of the first rank, spreading out the seven gifts on a daily basis, often for decades and to thousands of students. What child doesn't need to experience encouragement, energy, enthusiasm, empathy, good humor, graciousness, gratitude, and loads of patience?

People who have benefited from great teachers love to read or watch stories of great teachers. And they wonder if their lives are as significant as the lives of the teachers who bent the arcs of their own lives. Because I was blessed to be born into a family with two parents who stayed together their entire lives and for the first forty-three years of my life, I can't honestly say, as many can, that a teacher saved my life. But I know that many teachers shaped my life.

When it comes to teachers, I can name them all, as I suspect most of you can as well. From kindergarten to eighth grade:

K Mrs. Fitting
1 Sister Mary Columba
2 Mrs. Was
3 Sister Benedicta
4 Ms. Bokone (later Mrs. Layshock)
5 Mrs. LaRock
6 Sister Mary Neal
7 Mr. Santore
8 Sister Timothy, later Sister Rita May

And from my years at John F. Kennedy High School, where I must have had thirty different teachers, four stand out: Fred Hoover, Sister Mary Jean Konerko, Ron Karrenbauer, and Kathy Santucci. Fred Hoover taught me to love literature; Sister Mary Jean, geometry and trig; Ron Karrenbauer, Latin; and Kathy, how to figure out college applications. But all were much more than their fields of expertise. Each was a giver of extraordinary amounts of encouragement. Karrenbauer especially made it abundantly clear that any kid in America could go anywhere and do whatever he or she set out to do. I don't know that he ever gave that lecture, but he lived it.

Catholic education in the sixties and seventies was part of an overarching Catholic culture. The *New York Times*'s Ross Douthat wrote about this culture at length in his excellent 2012 book *Bad Religion*. To be born into that culture was to be guarded and nurtured in a particular fashion—a nearly complete meritocracy where achievement in either academics or sports, and preferably both, mattered more than anything else. My parents had bought into that system even though my dad was a Presbyterian, because my mom was a product of the even stricter Catholic culture of the twenties, thirties, and forties, the one familiar through Bing Crosby movies but which had made the immigrant experience in America a process in belonging and achieving.

That culture endured, as Douthat chronicled, until its collapse in the new century under the accumulated burdens of many sorts, but especially under the awful weight of the priest abuse scandals (one of which shook my old high school in 2013 after laying hidden for thirty years; the perpetrator arrived after I had been gone a few years, so I cannot say I would have noticed him or his crimes any earlier than those who were there at the time). That 95 percent of us products of Catholic education never met with other than dedicated priests, nuns, and lay professionals doesn't matter much in the look back in anger media of today.

But a wonderful Catholic culture existed, and it thrived and produced millions of productive, happy people. Oh, there were bumblers, and Catholic schools kept religious and lay teachers long past their primes, a reward for working without tenure and at 50 to 75 percent what they might have made in a public school system with a union. But they were dedicated, good-hearted people, and their commitment to the children they taught was complete, often all-encompassing, a vocation every bit as divine as that of any priest or doctor or nurse.

Public education of early postwar America had many of the same sort of professionals and functioned in much the same way until it, too, was overwhelmed by the cultural collapse of the last quarter-century of the American welfare state. The teachers didn't lose their drive or their desire to help kids. Their ability to do so, however, was severely truncated. Having sent three kids through thirteen years each of public education in California, I know firsthand that the vast number of teachers they had remain dedicated professionals and gift givers. I also know, however, that the modern public employee union has made it practically impossible to dismiss the 10 to 20 percent who can poison a school or an entire education. I also know that the public finance system takes enormous sums of money and squanders vast portions of it far from the classroom, and that the pension benefits negotiated over decades will cripple the system as surely as the sun sets in the west.

But nine out of ten teachers? Still amazing. Still sacrifice-oriented. Still doing what my teachers did and your teachers did.

I wrote Sister Mary Jean at her North Carolina high school where she is still working away with her students. I asked her simply if the students had given her anything back after fifty years of classroom teaching. She responded that she got back two things. First, a "desire to constantly grow in knowledge and methodology as a teacher, to be able to give more and encourage more." Okay, I thought, that makes sense. Students can challenge teachers to be better and better; and in improving their lives, the teacher can gain greater and greater satisfaction. It was the second gift she numbered that was surprising: "A deeper sense of humility," Sister Mary Jean wrote, "as I saw the potential in the men and women sitting before me."

This has a lot to do, I think, with C. S. Lewis's admonition quoted in the last chapter, about "immortal horrors or everlasting splendours." Teachers, over one year or fifty, are going to see a lot of the raw material of life. A lot of potential. A lot of waste. A lot of hope and a lot of suffering. They have twenty to forty mini-dramas playing out before them in every class, more than a hundred scripts being written every single day of their professional lives. It must be dizzying and thrilling and also deeply discouraging and almost despair inducing.

The impact lasts for years. Once, my call screener Marlon put through "Julie from Phoenix." Julie turned out to be Julie Dailey and introduced herself as a fellow graduate of Warren Kennedy High School. As I had been writing this chapter and had just had an e-mail from Sister Mary Jean, I asked if she had had the good sister. Julie replied, of course, honors biology, before adding that she had also spent four years of Latin and two of ancient Greek with Ron Karrenbauer, and honors English with Fred Hoover. We ragged on arch rival Howland High School a bit, and then moved to talk about the subject of her call.

Later that evening I mentioned to my son James how weird the timing of that call was. "A God thing" I called it, which is Christianspeak for coincidences that seem very well timed and about good things, a sort of small grace.

I followed up the next day by calling the high school to get Fred Hoover's number and spoke with him and then with Ron Karrenbauer. I sent them the same question I had sent Sister Mary Jean: What had they gotten out of their teaching careers? From Latin and Greek teacher Karrenbauer came a brief response in the same sort of cadence I can recall from forty years earlier:

> It may well be that there is more in common between the schoolman and the planter than one may initially think. Each must find receptive fields wherein he can only till the soil and plant the seed. If and when they take hold, he must root out the encroaching chaff while encouraging the growth of his crop. Yet all depends on the ambient light of the Son. If all goes

well and what has been planted does become awash in a flood of distraction, the farmer and the schoolman will witness the yield of their labors unexpected in common hours.

The "schoolman." How that turn of phrase captures a life-long commitment to the classroom.

From English teacher Hoover, a very differently phrased assessment:

To attempt to distill forty-four years of teaching seems an overwhelming task. Yet when reduced to the basic question of whether there was a return loop or whether the students gave back makes it much more intriguing than overpowering. Granted one cannot total the hours spent in the classroom or at the dining room table, grading, reading, analyzing, pondering, planning, and hoping. Yet the truth is that there is a reward system in place that offers much more to the teacher.

The student who struggles, whether in the classroom or with challenges in their personal life, to learn, to grow, to become educated is a reward both extrinsic and intrinsic. Throughout many years I presented information about language development, British Literature, American Literature, rules of grammar, expository writing, development of theses, collecting support as well as disagreement with the thesis, and finally molding all this into a presentation that was worthy of reading and discussion. The classroom discussions offered insight to young people who though seemingly disaffected or more in tune with the latest fad still sought knowledge and the opportunity to know on a personal level what had mattered to different societies throughout time. The smile of recognition and the budding realization that what mattered in 1967, 1977, 1987, 1997, 2007, and even in 2011 was really not that different than what had been discovered in the literature of earlier periods by people struggling with essentially the same problems and challenges that each generation confronts is a reward. For students to see and embrace the idea that they are intricately linked to the past as well as committed to a better future fosters a commitment to continue to improve the world around as well to make their own life better. I believe that in the proper context, any student is capable of mastering material that will help him/her later in life. This is the beginning of the extrinsic reward.

That reward that others see is marked in the smiles at graduation, the prayerful and thoughtful participation in a Baccalaureate Mass, and the joyous embrace shared with parents, family, and teachers. The reward continues as the former student takes her/his place in college, the workplace, or the community and continues to reflect the values and aspirations that have moved them thus far. When a student achieves acclaim and recognition, that is part of the extrinsic reward, too. To illustrate, I attended the wedding of a former student who had become a teacher and was teaching alongside me. At the reception, I commented to one of the other attendees who worked with the young man's new bride and offered that I was happy to see what he had become. The other guest replied that what he was probably [was] because of what had occurred in my classroom. That gave me pause and helped me understand that through the many years and hours, I had made an impact that may never be directly acknowledged. I had affected the future. This begins the intrinsic aspect.

Many times I have encountered former students, some of whom have had their children placed in my classroom, and have been told that they owe me more than they can ever pay. Their work life, their school success, their families have been affected by what happened in that classroom. This is something that I cannot take to the bank, nor can I spend it at the supermarket or hardware store. But it is mine to cherish and value as I pause to reflect. Personal reward, intrinsic reward, extrinsic reward ultimately mean little. When you approach the profession of teaching, challenged by the words of Jesus to "let these my little ones come to me . . . it were better to have a millstone placed around your neck and be cast into the sea rather than to give bad example to one of these my little ones," you accept an awesome responsibility and with that awesome task comes a concomitantly awesome reward. Many of my students have achieved great public acclaim, have made more money than I'll ever know, have written books, saved lives, lived good lives for their families, their children, their friends. They have been good neighbors, good friends, good employees. Some have been taken from this world too soon; some have less positive histories. Each of them is one of my students who gave me a chance to be important in their life. What more might I ask than that?

Note the obvious religious faith of the two men. The Catholic environment attracted very, very dedicated professionals, who worked for significantly less pay than their public school counterparts. Their colleagues in city school systems no doubt have the same love of students and love of teaching.

I'd be lying if I didn't confess some lingering skepticism about

Richard Dreyfuss's declaration. But with each year I grow more and more open to believing him. There are countless schools that can boast successful graduates, but all of them have one thing in common: great teachers. Communities that thrive and produce adults of character and accomplishment do so because they have schools staffed by the most dedicated professionals.

Those professionals rarely, if ever, get the honor and praise due them, or even a phone call from the students they nurtured a generation ago. This is the gift gap—and while with a little prompting we may try and fill gift gaps within our families, with our parents and coworkers, and within our churches, my guess is that fewer than one in ten thousand do so with regard to their teachers. So let that be a prompt, either to take a moment to find and thank those teachers, or to encourage the ones you know now in a world that is so much harder in which to succeed in this highest calling.

THE CHURCH

"Here are My mother and My brothers!"

—The Gospel of Matthew

RICK WARREN WAS SEATED IN A SMALL OFFICE IN A small shopping center off El Toro Road in 1990 when I first met him. The man who would become the most influential evangelical in the world through his church, Saddleback Valley Community Church, and through his book *The Purpose Driven Life*, which has sold close to fifty million copies, was not yet famous. Indeed, he didn't have a church building. He had a tent.

He did have some land. But it was the wrong land. And that's why I was there.

From the moment I returned to southern California after my time in the Reagan administration, I have practiced law—specifically the kind of lawyering required by the federal Endangered Species and Clean Water Acts. When those two laws impacted people's property because their land was home to a rare or soon-to-be-rare species, or because it was home to a wetland or "navigable waters" as defined by the federal government, I was there to help. I did that from 1989 onward. I'm still doing it. It is a unique skill set, and it has taken me all over the country.

I was in Rick's office because he had bought a site for his future church home that was covered in California gnatcatchers, an endangered bird. He discovered this after he had purchased the property—through no fault of his own. So Rick had big, big dreams and land he couldn't build them on. As he told me those dreams, I think I kept my skepticism off my face; at least I hope I did. But I know for a fact I did not think Rick needed as much land as he said he needed, or that his church could possibly grow the way he said it was going to grow.

Count me a successor in interest to Doubting Thomas. Rick Warren, of course, shattered all the doubts of all the skeptics. I was pleased to have helped play a very small role in finding a big new site for the church that stands today—one without gnatcatchers on it—and even more proud to have become Rick's friend, to have preached at his church, and to have hosted him on the radio show on many occasions, including after he gave the prayer at President Obama's historic first inauguration.

Rick's an amazing man, and his wife, Kay, an amazing woman. Their lives have been among the most significant of the last century, and when they suffered the tragic loss of their son in early 2013, a victim of the depression he had battled for many years, millions mourned with them and prayed for them.

The Warrens modeled for the world how to suffer the worst blow and still trust in God to lead them through every valley as He had during all their previous years. Their church, local and international, rallied to them as best anyone reeling from such a loss could be ministered to, enveloping them in love and prayer that Rick would tweet about throughout the days following their son's death. Though it was the farthest thing from Rick's mind, he was showing the world what true community was in his church's sharing his and Kay's sufferings.

It has been my great gift from God to have met and become friends with and to have interviewed not just Rick but many of the age's greatest pastors and theologians, as well as religious leaders from outside Christianity. It has also been my great gift to have been pastored by extraordinary people—Fathers Nist and DeCrane from my first memories to Father Tom Pado, my current priest, or Pastor Scott Bullock, my current pastor. All these amazing men and women of faith have impacted my professional life as well as my faith life. Archbishop Charles Chaput, now of Philadelphia but of Denver when I first met him, has had an enormous impact on my life. Like I said, blessed.

This vein in my journalistic career has been almost accidental. When I was first offered a weekend radio show by George Oliva at KFI's AM 640 in 1990, I didn't intend to spend much time on subjects related to faith. I began on Saturdays, from 11:00 a.m. to 2:00 p.m., following "the one, the only, the wrong" Bill Press, and stuck to news and politics for the first couple of years of weekend shows.

But as my kids went from infancy to elementary school, I did what most every dad in southern California did: I began to coach soccer and baseball and help at swim meets. I was a terrible soccer coach, something that the Orange Tigers, the Red Rockets, and Fighting Irish alums have never let me forget since I blew a playoff appearance by messing up the shootout and not using big-footed Bobby Rupert when I ought to have. I was an even worse baseball coach, but luckily Emmett Raitt handled the serious coaching, and I just hauled around the equipment. Swimming I knew, and stroke judging was up my alley. Still, all this occurred on Saturday mornings, so I arranged with KFI to switch to the Sunday night shift, from nine to midnight.

This is the graveyard shift, but with two great advantages. First, KFI was 50,000 watts of clear channel power, so I could blast out across the western United States and sometimes even be heard all the way to western North Carolina. This allowed for a huge, if eclectic, audience of late-nighters across the fruited plain.

Second, management never listened, so I could do whatever I wanted to do. The very first hour of the very first Sunday broadcast, I mined the divide between Protestants, Catholics, and Jews by asking if it made sense to pray for the dead.

I am the child of a mixed marriage: a devout Roman Catholic mom and a very dutiful Presbyterian elder. My mom and dad married in the era when the Catholic-Protestant couple stood at the side altar and also signed a form pledging that the kids would be raised Catholic, and we were. But Dad always stayed Presbyterian and always went off to his church on Sunday mornings while we went off to our Roman Catholic Mass; my brothers, Bill and John, and I attended Catholic schools through twelfth grade. Pops would come to Christmas and Easter Mass with us, but we never ever went to the Presbyterian church with him.

Perhaps this made me susceptible to religious debates. It

wasn't a matter of contention in my home growing up, but just the way it was done. Dad was the favorite Protestant of the Catholics of Warren, coaching the Catholic elementary school basketball team, leading the high school boosters for a time, and serving two decades on the board of the Catholic hospital, including two terms as its chair. Bill Hewitt was beloved of the nuns who ran the hospital, a group of hard-nosed businesswomen, for many reasons, not the least of them because each Christmas he brought them cases of wine and nothing else as a seasonal gift. Marguerite Hewitt was the Catholic, but Bill Hewitt was the go-to guy.

I suspect my own faith journey is just the product of this divided religious DNA. I was a faithful Catholic until about 1992. All our three children were baptized Catholic, but the bishops of those years went further and further left—how the absurd letters on nuclear weapons and economics from the American bishops had annoyed me in the eighties, signed by Bishop Jim Malone who confirmed me and knew as much about either subject as I knew about Cordon Bleu cooking. But I hung in.

About that time I went to a men's retreat, had a profound experience of God, and signed on with the evangelicals exclusively for a long time, mentored in my faith by a wonderful pair of Presbyterian pastors, Ben Patterson and Mark D. Roberts, and living out my curiosity about ultimate issues on air on Sunday nights, often inviting men and women of the faith to talk about the subject.

At one point I read the whole of C. S. Lewis's *Mere Christianity* over the air on successive Sunday nights. The book had been delivered as a series of lectures by Lewis on the BBC during World War II, so it made sense to me. The audience loved it as well, especially the community of Wiccans who lived on Big Bear, a mountain community in California, who were prolific callers to radio shows on late Sunday nights.

From these broadcasts came a phone call from the wonderful Martin Burns, a producer with KCET TV, the then–PBS affiliate in Los Angeles, in late 1991. Would I be interested in auditioning for a nightly news and public affairs show, to be named *Life & Times*, which would air Monday through Friday nights?

Why not? And thus was launched a television career that would begin in February 1992 (just in time for the Los Angeles riots two months later) and continue until I had to lay down the television gig when the national radio show moved to afternoons in 2002.

The decade I did local television featured a lot of reporting on faith. I made it a specialty. I sold the producers in doing a special, which I hosted, on the Harvest Crusade's Greg Laurie, which put up audience numbers that stunned the staff. When the great Rabbi Adin Steinsaltz, an amazing man of God and teacher of Talmud, came through town, I sat him down in both television and radio studios to talk about the big things. When New Age flowered, I sat down James Redfield of *Celestine Prophecy* fame. Martin and Saul Gonzales were extraordinary producers, and they lived to plumb this interest of mine. So we did, and the audience loved it as well, even as the aftermath of riots and the Clinton years unfolded and we covered politics top to bottom.

I gave up the radio in 1992 because my family needed more of my time. Three young children wanted their dad around on Sunday afternoons and evenings, as did the Fetching Mrs. Hewitt. This wasn't a hard decision in the least. First God, then spouse, then children, especially when they are young. That approach means that now as I head into late middle age and they are on their own, we love and cherish each other and spend time together. The choice to give up radio was actually a choice to put family first. If my kids take nothing else away from this book, it is that that choice was the best I ever made, and the best kind you will ever make.

I kept up with my law practice and television work, and devoted my faith life exclusively to our Presbyterian church, serving on the session, and distressing my mom greatly (though not my dad, who smiled, I think, that he had a co-religionist in the family at last). Going into the deep dive made me a very different Christian, as it meant different approaches to Scripture and different reading regimens; but the Catholic heart still beat. More on that coming.

In 1994, the GOP swept the congressional elections in a stunner. I hosted the live coverage on KCET that night and opened the show with an unscripted, "If this was a fight, they'd stop it!" Then Congressman Chris Cox arrived as a guest and spoke the truth: anyone who said they saw this coming was lying, as no one had predicted the rise of Newt to Speaker.

Certainly not the Pooh-Bahs at PBS. As I noted in an earlier chapter, a few days after the smoke cleared, a phone rang in the office of Bill Kobin, the president of KCET, a call that came from DC headquarters suddenly very concerned with "balance" on the network. Didn't Bill have a conservative on-air talent? Yes, he did—Hugh Hewitt. Would Hugh Hewitt like to host a national show? Bill agreed to ask. The budget was $500,000, a hefty sum in 1994–1995 PBS dollars.

I, of course, said yes, and to my surprise they asked me what I would like to do. I instantly, really, without thinking, said God.

I can try and recall why from the distance of two decades, but it is hazy. I just knew it interested me, and from all the time I had spent on the subject on radio and television in the previous five years, I knew it would interest the audience. Thus was born *Searching for God in America,* an eight-part series that aired in the summer of 1996, conversations I had with eight very different religious leaders mentioned earlier.

Of the eight interviews, the one that most affected my broadcasting life was my two days taping and talking with Elder Neal Maxwell of the Church of Jesus Christ of Latter-day Saints. I am not now, nor have I ever been, a Mormon. I didn't know much about the faith when I arranged the interview with Elder Maxwell, which took place in Brigham Young's Beehive House in Salt Lake City. To prepare for the interview I did as much research as I could, and read widely on Mormon theology and anti-Mormon apologetics. Then I spent days with Elder Maxwell, who is among the best men I have ever met, one of the kindest, most gracious, deeply loving, and compassionate souls I have crossed paths with.

"Elder Maxwell, you and I are never going to agree on theology," I said in an exchange that did not survive the final cut. "We believe different things, but I want to know what you believe and why."

In an exchange that did survive, I said, "In one respect, I as a Presbyterian, you as a Mormon, both believe extraordinary things."

In these and other exchanges and throughout the interview, I was trying to communicate to him—and did—that I was not a prosecutor of his beliefs but a reporter of what they were. This attitude of non-confrontation helped begin a friendship that endured and deepened so that when PBS in Utah wanted to make a special about this extraordinary man's life, Elder Maxwell requested that I host it, which I gladly did. I was a guest in his home and a telephone friend on all sorts of political issues. He was a political junkie and we enjoyed reviewing the give-and-take of politics.

We never talked theology off-camera. We just knew we didn't agree. But he was a friend indeed, and that friendship led me to write a book about Mitt Romney in 2006. Because I knew the level of anti-Mormon bigotry in this country, I suspected that the then-governor of Massachusetts, Mitt Romney, would run into some unique problems if he ran for president, as was widely speculated. I had never met, or even interviewed, Romney, but I thought the idea of a book about a Mormon running a serious race for the White House would be interesting. It also merged with my academic research and teaching that had focused on the Religion Clauses of the First Amendment and the prohibition on religious texts embodied in Article VI of the Constitution.

My publisher agreed, and after a few stone walls were broken down, the governor received me in his Massachusetts State House offices for the first of several interviews. A book was launched and a friendship begun that influenced the next eight years of my professional career. I became a Romney backer after I got to know the man, who, along with Richard Nixon and John Roberts, ranks among the most capable and intelligent men I have ever met.

That was all in the future when I sat down with Elder Maxwell for a PBS production in 1995, but lives follow arcs that are not obvious as they unfold.

The PBS series was critically acclaimed and led to book

offers including the companion book that came out with the series—transcripts of the interviews themselves and a compendium of the best American writing on faith I could assemble—and then my first book on faith, *The Embarrassed Believer*, which chronicled how religious belief in America had been marginalized, and how the Christian community had cooperated in that marginalization.

There was a market for books and conversations about God, serious but not boring, broad-spectrum not narrow casting. I followed the two books with a third, *In, But Not Of: A Guide to Christian Ambition and the Desire to Influence the World*, a book for young adults that remains the book people most often reference when we meet. It has affected many lives, which is both deeply satisfying and somewhat scary. Authors write to be read, and some to be influential. When it happens, you have to live with the consequences. Thus far, though, I have heard only good stories of how the book sent people off in directions that turned out to be good for them and honoring of God.

It was my public television work that birthed my current radio show. Throughout the years I've covered 70 percent politics and news, 25 percent faith and culture, and 5 percent the Cleveland Browns, Indians, Cavs, Ohio State Buckeyes, and Notre Dame Fighting Irish. I think it's a good mix. As it's primarily a show about national and international affairs, I cannot devote the show entirely, or even mostly, to God. But the thirst is so great for talk about God that it confirms this key lesson for me.

Everyone—every single person reading this and every person in the world—needs to belong to a church no matter whether they believe or not. They need to do so because the questions asked and debated in churches are the most important questions; they have been asked since the beginning of time for the simple reason that we are made to wonder about this world and our places in it. Those questions and that wondering are not served—reliably and seriously—anywhere except in a church. And thus that deep, deep hunger is fed only through life within a body devoted to answering these enormous questions of why the world is the way it is and how we ought to live in it.

I have belonged to many churches in my fifty-seven years, beginning with St. Pius X in Warren, Ohio, and most recently to both a Presbyterian congregation and a Catholic parish. I hear at least a hundred sermons a year, and the act of listening to a priest or a pastor expound on Scripture is always good, even if the sermon isn't. The point is the gift the church gives its members is a regular occasion for concentration on the biggest questions of them all.

The second gift a church gives is a community of people—far from like-minded and usually very diverse in terms of social and economic backgrounds—who are inclined to care about these big questions and because of that inclination to act in particularly civil ways. Real communities are very hard to come by. Workplaces are organized for profit, and neighborhoods are far from the stable, multi-relational centers of life they were even a few decades ago. Not so the church. "Nobody does small town better than a big church," the pastor of Columbia, South Carolina's First Baptist told me when I was there to speak after *The Embarrassed Believer* came out. He was right, of course; and the growth of the megachurch in America owed a lot to the desire for a hypermobile population to anchor themselves in familiar surroundings with presumably good people.

Church begins by offering the gifts of important conversations and real community, but for those who stay longer than a few weeks, it soon begins to teach the giving of the seven gifts by encouraging those who attend to participate, even occasionally, in various activities that teach gift giving, whether it is something as simple as teaching Sunday school to three-year-olds or helping out with the ushering, or second-level gift giving of dollar contributions or mission work, or third-level commitments of fellowship in a small group or an international mission. A healthy church will be all about gift giving and learning to give. And before you know it, you will be both giving and receiving in quantities you had never ever imagined.

Energy, enthusiasm, and gratitude—three of the seven gifts outlined in the first half of this book—should be evident in every worship service, even the most contemplative. Prayer and singing, the readings and indeed every aspect of church, whether Roman Catholic or Protestant, should be infused with these gifts, though, of course, we are susceptible to "going through the motions." The great worship director or liturgist, the terrific priest-homilist or preacher will be known for the energy and enthusiasm in proclaiming the gospel, and every participant will at least say the words of gratitude that are at the heart of every Christian service, thus setting the tone for a week ahead lived in accordance with the practices of collective worship.

When moderating a panel at my thirty-fifth Harvard College reunion on the varieties of religious experience among my classmates (more on that reunion in the conclusion) a question came from Mickey, who asked whether there are any benefits to participation in a faith community for the nonbeliever.

When my turn came to reply, I added two to the long list my

copanelists had detailed (such as life in community and collective action on issues of social justice).

First, I told the audience of my trip to Biola University with Christopher Hitchens and his dry "Here I am, in the den of lambs" quip that not only was funny but also reflected the undeniable fact that Biola was a very welcoming place full of very nice people, much like most—though not all—churches. Church, I assured my very—though not exclusively—secular audience would be full of very nice people, by which I mean empathetic, good-humored, gracious folk who would gladly share life's journey, with all its ups and downs, with them. This has been my experience and the experience of nearly everyone else I know who has genuinely committed themselves as an adult to a faith community and invested themselves within it.

As noted earlier, not long ago a group of my Presbyterian church members winged off to South Africa on a missions trip to the three ministries our church supports financially there, including one program that simply feeds children who would otherwise not get fed. The group from our church included, not surprisingly, our pastor, but also a senior partner in a major law firm, an investment banker, a very experienced accountant, and two stay-at-home moms. They came back transformed by their weeks among the very poor, and with a deep bond between themselves that inspired the church to undertake to send dozens of our members to the same ministry for the same purposes of encouragement and being encouraged in 2014.

This is routine. *Routine.* It happens in almost every church I know of, and not just among those who undertake far-flung missions work, but also among those who help organize the Vacation Bible School, the young moms group, the Angel Tree program of

Prison Fellowship, or the Operation Shoebox collection effort founded by Franklin Graham and operated through a network of thousands of churches. Each of these and thousands more programs and ministries do good for the lost and the least and transform the participants as well.

No one has to believe anything to be a part of such a community, though faith can be infectious.

The second thing I mentioned to my Harvard audience is that generosity is a learned behavior, but that it is not inevitably learned, and that they and their children could and would learn it in most churches if they attended regularly. (Later a dear friend, Julie, took me aside to tell me that the private schools of Manhattan quite seriously and comprehensively championed service and generosity, which is a very good thing. But Julie had to concede that this is a rare thing to see carried out comprehensively in most public schools.) The habits of giving and volunteering that are part and parcel of almost every Sunday school in the country do not go unabsorbed by the children on whom they are conferred and to whom they are modeled.

How much happier people would be if, regardless of their beliefs, they showed up at the same church most every Sunday, said the same prayers, chatted with the same people, heard the same sermons, attended the same potlucks.

Listen to me. This is the key to renewing your life if you are unhappy. Pick a church. Practically any church. Go and go and go again and again and again. Even if you are shy, force yourself to say hello to the greeter and find a second gathering there—a Bible study, a class, a lecture—and go again. After a month you will have seamlessly evolved into a churchgoer and your life will be almost inestimably better.

There are huge theological divisions between churches, but they hardly matter if you are unchurched. Here's my advice: pick the biggest church within five miles of your apartment or house and just go there. Stick there for a year. Then decide if you need to change because of theology. If you are a cradle Catholic, find your closest Catholic parish. Familiarity will make the first few visits easier on you even if you are shy beyond belief.

People want to talk about God and about this crazy world with all its terrors and pains. And people do talk about God and about this crazy world with all its terrors and pains, every Sunday and often throughout the week.

So go.

When you do, send me an e-mail and tell me about it: hugh@hughhewitt.com. I have asked this before on the radio show and gotten e-mails in response. Never one that regretted going. Trust me on this. It's a real game changer.

THE GREATEST GIVER

Every good and perfect gift is from above.

—THE EPISTLE OF JAMES (NIV)

EVERYTHING IN THIS BOOK IS JUST WINDOW-DRESSING if Jesus Christ is who He says He is, and if He did what Scripture says He did. All books except the Bible are. As are all things—most certainly politics and talk radio, but everything that is not the simple declaration of the gospel.

Do not get me wrong. Politics and debate are important. Media is important. All work and all of life are important. But only in relationship to God and Christ. Genuine importance is the measurement of activity only in its relationship to the gospel. The gospel is the measuring stick of all human activity.

One of the greatest Christian intellects ever, Thomas Aquinas, had a revelation near the end of his life that was so powerful, so life-changing, he quit writing. Even finishing his crowning work, the *Summa Theologica*, was off the table. His friend and secretary, Reginald, asked him about it. "The end of my labors has come," answered Thomas, according to Alban Butler's *Lives of the Saints*. "All that I have written appears to be as so much straw after the things that have been revealed to me." Reginald later pushed him again, but the saint responded, "I can write no more. I have seen things that make my writings like straw."

I try to remind myself of the absurdity of our attempts at significance most days and of the essential priority of Jesus. Then I forget it and live in the world, and then try to remind myself of it at night before sleeping. This feeble thing is called a prayer life.

I can go weeks and months without recollecting this basic truth about priority. This is why I think the Roman Catholic Church puts such a premium on weekly attendance at Mass. Yes, the obligation to attend Mass on Sundays and holy days of obligation reflects love of God and facilitates the occasion of grace through the sacrament. But it is also a prod to at least notice the huge theme of history, or the here and now, and of your life on a weekly basis. Everything else matters only to the extent it is in sync with the basic truth of Jesus entering history and sacrificing Himself so that we can participate in the coming kingdom. Getting people into the church and looking up and out of their own drama is key to this.

Not that it always works. I confess to having spent many a Mass thinking about many other things besides the Mass. I have spent thousands of hours in church not thinking about God. But there's a much better chance of focusing if you go than if you don't. And when you focus, there is a chance the big truth will recur to you, or perhaps even arrive in its fullness for the first time.

My favorite all-time quote—big statement for someone like me who loves quotes—is from evangelist D. L. Moody:

> Some day you will read in the papers that D. L. Moody of East Northfield is dead. Don't you believe a word of it! At that moment I shall be more alive than I am now; I shall have gone up higher, that is all, out of this old clay tenement into a house that is immortal—a body that death cannot touch, that sin cannot taint; a body fashioned like unto His glorious body.
>
> I was born of the flesh in 1837. I was born of the Spirit in 1856. That which is born of the flesh may die. That which is born of the Spirit will live forever.

Moody was an under-schooled boy who later became a Boston shoe salesman. Then he found Christ. He stayed in business but started organizing a Sunday school program and later a church. He finally quit business to focus on ministry and became famous for his charity efforts, evangelism, and educational initiative, including the establishment of several theological and trade schools.

How I would have loved to interview Moody. As noted earlier, I have interviewed, at length and often, great evangelists like Greg Laurie, Franklin Graham, and Luis Palau. I have interviewed incredible theologians like Dr. Albert Mohler, Dr. Mark D. Roberts, and Philadelphia archbishop Charles Chaput. These and many others are great men of faith, witnesses to truth, fearless and bold, and we are lucky to have them in this age.

Moody, in that one quote, communicated a confidence, an optimism, a vibrant exploding faith that all these other great and good witnesses continually communicate and that the world needs so much today. Moody, in that one quote, pierces hearts with Christian certainty, the enemy of the Enemy's greatest weapons, which are doubt and fear. In that one quote is granite-hard and diamond-brilliant certainty. It is the balm of the age, and it is in woefully short supply.

Some opponents of faith—and I have debated most of the famous ones; these debates are compiled in my e-book *Talking with Pagans*—wish to condemn all religious certainty, citing the certainty that drives Islamist terrorists or the long-ago Inquisition. This is a straw man argument. The biggest, driest of them all, the Burning Man of Straw Men. Today's Christianity, the right and proper understanding of the gospel of peace, is no threat to anyone. Its most certain practitioners are spread out across the world doing good, and doing good regardless of the faiths of those who receive that good.

Back to Moody. Moody had no business presuming to try and change anyone's life, much less the lives of millions, much less the world. He was, I repeat, a shoe salesman when he set out on his mission.

I stress Moody's ordinary original vocation because we all have ordinary vocations. Really, all of us. None of us are doing anything that will matter in the blink of an eye. All success is gone in a moment. The titans of the age will be footnotes in a quarter or at most a half century, forgotten in two. Even a figure as significant as President Obama will in time be a boring textbook entry for seventh graders. Caesar didn't last beyond the attention of a relatively few people who love history. No one will. A love of history grants you recognition that everyone's pretensions to significance are absurd.

The planet is billions of years old. There have been humans

on it for a very brief time, and God made a lot of us and is making more for reasons that are utterly beyond our understanding. We do not get what is going on, though we are very much supposed to get—and to do—our part in it.

Think of yourself as a bit character in a massive Russian novel. Maybe even a bit bigger than a bit character, but still a character. You don't know your part in the plot, and you won't ever know it this side of heaven; but you do know, or ought to know, how to act in whatever set of circumstances comes your way.

In recent years there were two very popular television series: *24*, the adventures of Jack Bauer, played by Kiefer Sutherland; and *Friday Night Lights*, the adventures of Coach Eric Taylor, played by Kyle Chandler.

In both series—the first a national security thriller and the other the life of a Texas high school football coach—the main characters were continually confronted with difficult moral choices: Does Jack Bauer use force in interrogating a terrorist? Does Coach Taylor play or suspend a star running back who used steroids? The drama in both shows, every week, was in the moral choices of the lead characters and in the choices of their costars.

Moral choices occur in every life with regularity and at least occasionally on a dramatic scale. No matter how big the stage, they are the most significant parts of life. They ought to be informed by and guided by the gospel as the individual understands the gospel.

Of course that doesn't mean agreement. I have argued long and hard with my coreligionists on many issues and will as long as I am able to. I think some things are very, very clear that they think are quite obviously wrong. That isn't going to change.

But the desire to argue from first principles is changing.

Some arguments have become so heated—over marriage, for example—that there is little space left for anything like reasoned debate. The volume, duration, and emotional heat of those arguments have begun to destroy the capacity of some people to even see the potential for good in those across the aisle.

This is a nightmare. In our private lives there is always space for the gifts I have been writing about, regardless of political differences; and to me the key to all politics is the just distribution of those gifts by individuals to individuals, regardless of political views, party, or heartfelt agenda. There is, for Christians, at least, but I suspect for all men and women of any sincere moral system, an obligation to give the gifts touched on in the earlier chapters, to do so in all the relationships numbered, and to do so generously.

That obligation is found in various places in the Scripture, but let me give you just three. The first is from the sixth chapter of Micah:

> He has shown you, O man, what is good;
> And what does the LORD require of you
> But to do justly,
> To love mercy,
> And to walk humbly with your God? (v. 8)

Then this from the fourth chapter of Luke's Gospel, Jesus' first sermon:

> And Jesus returned in the power of the Spirit into Galilee, and a report about him went out through all the surrounding country. And he taught in their synagogues, being glorified

by all. And he came to Nazareth, where he had been brought up; and he went to the synagogue, as his custom was, on the Sabbath day. And he stood up to read; and there was given to him the book of the prophet Isaiah. He opened the book and found the place where it was written, "The Spirit of the Lord is upon me, because he has anointed me to preach good news to the poor. He has sent me to proclaim release to the captives and recovering of sight to the blind, to set at liberty those who are oppressed, to proclaim the acceptable year of the Lord."

And he closed the book, and gave it back to the attendant, and sat down; and the eyes of all in the synagogue were fixed on him.

And he began to say to them, "Today this scripture has been fulfilled in your hearing." (vv. 14–21 RSV)

And finally this, from the twelfth chapter of the epistle to the Hebrews:

See to it that no one falls short of the grace of God and that no bitter root grows up to cause trouble and defile many. (v. 15 NIV)

Everything I have learned in all these years of broadcasting is that kindness is just, cruelty is unjust, and fairness is quite easily recognized, understood, and acted upon. I have that understanding due to my attending church for more than fifty years and listening to constant repetitions of the same readings and the same messages. That is what is wonderful about faithful church attendance. Something gets through. Something sticks.

If I had any theological chops at all, I could now tell you how grace is God's gift, variously delivered through the agencies of

Jesus, the Holy Spirit, and the sacraments, and the gifts we give each other are simply the poor human imitations of the various graces we receive.

But I don't. So I commend you to the works of the people cited above and many, many others. If you are persuaded by anything I have suggested in any of these chapters, please understand that it is because I heard the one big truth long ago and have been listening for it ever since, in almost every interview with almost every guest. At least that is the case when I am doing my best work.

CONCLUSION

ARTHUR BROOKS IS AN ECONOMIST, OR SO HE SAYS. HE is actually a moral philosopher who began as a French horn player—the professional symphony member sort—then became an economist. He is the president of one of the very best think tanks around, the American Enterprise Institute. He is also the author of a wonderful book, *The Road to Freedom,* which I cannot recommend highly enough. He has been my guest on air many, many times.

Larry Kudlow interviewed Arthur in front of the audience attending the National Review Institute in late January 2013. The conference had featured many inspirational figures, both public intellectuals like Maggie Gallagher, Charles Krauthammer, Bill Kristol, and John Podhoretz, along with elected leaders like Ted Cruz, Bobby Jindal, Paul Ryan, and Scott Walker.

Arthur stole the show, something for which think tank presidents are hardly famous. I know Arthur stole the show because I took my son with me to this conference, and he told me so. This was son James, then a senior in college. His brother, Will, was finishing his student teaching and preparing for his first season as a head swim coach, and his sister and her husband and baby were half a world away, or I would have asked them all to come.

Conferences of conservatives arguing about the future are actually a lot of fun, especially when Jonah Goldberg, Rob Long, and Mark Steyn are doing their late-night comedy routine after the banquet featuring Bill Bennett delivering an inspiring message of coming back from political defeat. (This was just two months after a loss many felt as shattering because, like me, they not only thought Mitt Romney was a good man and would be a very good president, but also were worried for the country.)

Only James could make it, though, and on Sunday morning Larry and Arthur delivered an hour's conversation that every parent, right or left, would want all of his or her children to hear. It was a talk about happiness, and the path to happiness.

It isn't about money. Our celebrity- and consumption-driven culture makes this very hard to hear, much less believe, but it is true. Rather, Arthur argued, citing numerous studies by the best academics in the world, it is about having at least two or three of the big four: faith, family, community, and fulfilling work.

Of course, four out of four increases the odds of happiness, and bad things can still happen to good people—illness and accident arrive out of left field and can upset even the happiest of lives—but Brooks was talking in the broad generalities that apply to millions and tens of millions and hundreds of millions of Americans.

Faith, family, community, and fulfilling work. That is it. Aim for these things.

Develop your faith life by consistent practice, reading Scripture, attending services.

Sacrifice everything for family and not just immediate family but extended family. Keep them close. Spend time with them. Always put them first. When you marry, do the work to stay married.

Friends matter. A lot. Value and serve them. Seek new ones and cling to old ones. Work alongside them for the good of the community. Do not betray them or neglect them.

And find something to do that you enjoy doing, adjusting your consumption to your income so that you can, in fact, do that work which gives you pleasure and fulfillment.

All these things add up to what Arthur brands as "earned success," and earned success is the essential ingredient of happiness.

Arthur also noted the research that objectively calculated the age in which a man is most likely to be most unhappy. (He was quite definitive as well as to its applying to men and not women, for a variety of reasons; but the lesson drawn from it applies to both sexes.)

Men are most likely to be unhappiest at the age of forty-five, and not because of dropping testosterone levels. It is at that age when they realize they may have missed what Arthur called the "off ramp" to happiness: they may have driven past the chance for family, for deep friendship, for the sort of work that saw them spring up in the morning, eager to begin a new day, and for a real relationship with God.

Though Arthur did not say so, this feeling of unhappiness is based on a false premise of age equaling inevitability. In fact, many millions of people find faith or friends, renewed family bonds or a new career after forty-five; but it is harder to do because of previous choices. This difficulty in imagining and practical implementation is what pushes down the happiness meter.*

What James found so inspiring about Arthur's message was his certainty about the ability to try and try and try to get life right, the exuberance he displayed in talking about the opportunities that free societies offer everyone to pick up after failure and begin again. Most countries throughout human history have denied most people this basic chance to dream and act.

Arthur's second point was that human happiness is inextricably bound up with doing good. Because we are born with a conscience, action opposite that conscience's understanding of the good produces profound unhappiness. The best way to achieve happiness is to do good for others—starting with the seven gifts we've talked about here. The best guarantee of deep unhappiness is to do injury. In truth, all you have to do to ensure your misery is be stingy with the seven gifts.

Doing good can, of course, mean doing very hard things, even as soldiers do in combat or police in their work. But even the hardest things can bring satisfaction and deep happiness if done rightly for the right reasons. The soldiers who toppled the Taliban or overthrew the butcher, Saddam, had to kill to accomplish that; but they brought freedom to the oppressed and the possibility of better lives to millions through their actions.

---

*Arthur did not say it, but Larry Kudlow referred to the other most common destroyer of happiness: addiction. Larry is a recovering alcoholic, outspoken about his disease and no doubt a source of inspiration to many thousands who have battled the disease and won, a battle that begins with one day of sobriety and a call to AA, a story Larry will tell whenever asked. If a reader has that problem, he or she should put everything else aside and go to an AA meeting this very day, and keep going for as long as it takes to remove the biggest obstacle to happiness. As Larry will tell you—as well as Bob Beckel and many other folks who have crossed my path over the years—it works, it is welcoming, and it isn't embarrassing in the least to show up at a place where a score of people are suffering from the same disease and have figured out for the most part how to deal with it.

I have known many soldiers, sailors, airmen, and Marines. Among them are some of the happiest, most fulfilled people I have ever met. Theirs are lives of high honor and incredible sacrifice, and they have often given more than any civilian can even imagine, and seen suffering on a scale that would stun the most cynical man or woman.

This living in the midst of great sacrifice and incredible suffering for the longest period of time is what makes Washington and Lincoln our greatest Americans, and how Churchill defined greatness in the twentieth century. Their "earned success" was in the midst of the greatest drama possible—the fate of their entire country—but their choices came down to the same decisions every person makes about selflessness every day, earning their own success every day. Very few people outside of combat have the challenge or the opportunity to lay down their lives for a friend, but everyone has the opportunity to give these incredible gifts.

I began this book in the year that three of my good friends— Tom Fuentes, Jerry Kushner, and Jerry Tardie—died, in a tough year politically and professionally, especially watching a very, very good man, Mitt Romney, lose the presidency at a time when the country and the world very much needed his abilities and leadership.

It was also, however, the first year of my first grandchild's life, which, as almost every grandparent will tell you, is wild with unique joys, and the year that my faith deepened and grew as my youngest finished college and all three of my children seemed to be making the good choices that mature adults would make. Betsy and I find this to be among the most satisfying of moments.

We also celebrated our thirtieth wedding anniversary, and

since we have enough good friends and colleagues who are not so fortunate, we appreciate that blessing and our marriage in ways we never have before. We have our aches and illnesses, and they will certainly increase; but modern medicine and good doctors are wonderful in ameliorating the problems. It looks as though I will succeed in continuing the broadcasting, teaching, and lawyering career I have loved so much. I may even be able to get back below four and a half hours in a marathon. In all, I can hardly imagine a better time to write a self-reflective book on the meaning of happiness and significance.

A. T. Rohl was a big figure in my life, my maternal grandfather, the fire chief of Ashtabula. Imagine what novelist Patrick O'Brian called in his Jack Aubrey–Stephen Maturin novels "the moral advantage" of being a little kid with a fire chief gramps.

He lived to be nearly a hundred and one and, until he took a tumble, lived alone past one hundred. He did so powered by bourbon and cigars.

Lulie Taussig was my wife's maternal grandmother, and she made it to ninety-nine, a widow for forty-two years, living in a building well known in Washington, DC—the Dresden—from 1946 forward, losing her husband, a somewhat famed figure in naval circles, Joe Taussig, in 1947. She, too, liked to smoke and drink Scotch.

It really does come down to the genes.

I wonder what A. T. and Lulie thought of the world and their lives in 1946, when they were both roughly the age I am now, when their children had left, or soon were to leave. Their daily lives, and their country, had survived perilous times full of sorrow and pain only to stumble into new eras of new challenges. How I would have loved to have a letter from them from that time, telling me what had mattered to them and how and why they had lived as they had.

Both were, to our knowledge, very happy people. Both had married young, stayed married, raised loving children, supported them, served their friends and churches and communities. Everything has changed, of course, and nothing at all. That is the biggest takeaway of all for every reader, and especially for my grandchildren, if they get this far someday, making their way through dated references and hopelessly archaic formulations. And for their grandchildren as well, no matter where or when they live or the trials and terrors of their age.

I was wrapping up this book when I went back to Harvard for only the third time in thirty-five years. Conservative intellectuals, authors, and talk show hosts are not much in demand on the campus as speakers or panel participants (nor at my law school, the University of Michigan, to which I have returned only once in thirty years) so I have only gone back for reunions.

Not much changes at Harvard, though my commencement speaker had been Solzhenitsyn and the class of '13 got Oprah. This sense of mission (and the sense, sometimes justified, sometimes not, of self-importance) is all around the campus and is infused into most of the alums. The institution has a $35 billion endowment (the next closest is Yale's with $20 billion) and a long, long list of the most distinguished in every field, though in recent decades its contributions to the leadership of the military and faith communities has not been pronounced.

So what makes the alumni of such a place happy? I asked many of my fellow reunion goers that very question, using this book as an excuse to be nosey and playing into the inevitable mood of self-assessment and reflection that accompanies such gatherings. Though we were only, on average, fifty-seven, we knew that many were already in the fourth quarter of their lives, and all of us at least well into the second halves. At fifty-seven you have a pretty good understanding of what life holds for you in the future, and hopefully a pretty clear view backward of what mattered most and what did genuinely produce happiness in the years gone by.

Family and friends were the common denominator, faith figured into many accounts of genuine happiness, and while the circumstances differed as to the specific institution—the New York City Botanical Gardens, Orange Lutheran High School, Harvard itself for a few who simply love the institution with an abandon—all these people and places and things were beloved by my classmates not because of what they had given to the men and women I had asked, but because my friends had been able to give to them, to become a part of them, to be generous toward them.

No one, not even the people with whom I have been the very closest of friends for nearly forty years, who would be completely honest with me, referred even once to anything having to do with money or assets. As I run through the list of my friends from before, during, and after college who were not there at the reunion, I can say with complete confidence—100 percent confidence—that none of them would count material accomplishment as that which brought them happiness. This is a pretty large cross-section of people from a very diverse set of backgrounds who have pursued a great variety of careers in places all over the country and indeed the world. None of them, not one, would say that their greatest happiness came from the things they had gotten. All of them would point to the people and institutions to whom they had given.

It is all about the giving: that which you have received from God and that which you give in His name. And if you have forgotten that, recall it. If you have failed, start again. If you are happy, be thankful. And if you aren't, you can be.

ACKNOWLEDGMENTS

THE CHAPTER ON GRATITUDE NOTES MANY OF THE people to whom I owe thanks and continuous expressions of public appreciation, as do many of the other chapters. To those I add only the names of Joel Miller who edited this book and Craig Wiley who, as my agent, found it a home; Lynne Chapman who kept it organized and Snow Philip who proofed it; and, of course, the Fetching Mrs. Hewitt who encouraged it, as she does me, every day of its making.

This is the place where I could have indulged in print my great love for the many good friendships with which I have been blessed. It is an exercise you ought to try, a simple listing of those people whom you really could denominate as a genuine friend. There is a hierarchy of friendship, and Aristotle calls out the categories, but here I am talking about the best sort of friends.

"The man therefore who is to come up to our notion of 'Happy,'" concludes Aristotle in the fourth chapter of book nine of the *Nicomachean Ethics*, "will need good friends."

I have them, and have had them from the earliest of my memories right through this moment, but decided not to print this list for fear of giving injury to anyone who thought themselves a friend but whom I overlooked or simply forgot. I would rather not give a bow to many friends than to unwittingly hurt one. Anyone who is my genuine friend will understand that if you think you would have been on that list, really and truly, thank you.

INDEX

A

Achoa, Anthony, 67

acknowledgments page in books, 58–59

Act of Valor (movie), 57

action, from empathy, 34

Adams, John, 104

addiction, as happiness destroyer, 160n

Afghanistan, Combat Outpost (COP) Keating, 33

Agresto, John, 67

Alcoholics Anonymous, 37–38

Alter, Jonathan, 64

ambition, 111

American Enterprise Institute, 7, 157

Anderson, Greg, 68, 109

Andrews, Julie, 40

anonymous charity, xxiii

arguments, 154

Aristotle, *Nicomachean Ethics*, xii

Armstrong, Bill, 113

Arnn, Larry, xiii–xiv, 113

Atlantic, 21

Atsinger, Ed, 67, 108

B

Beckel, Bob, 160n

Bendetti, Donald, 67

Benedict XVI (pope), *The Spirit of the Liturgy*, 27

Benedicta (sister), 124

Bennett, Bill, 108

Bergman, Alan, 76

Bergman, Marilyn, 76

Bible

  Micah 6:8, 154

  Luke 4:14–21, 154–155

  1 Corinthians, 104

  Hebrews 12:15, 155

Blecksmith, J. P., 33

Bokone, Ms., 67, 124

Book of Running (Fixx), 26

books

  acknowledgments page in, 58–59

  number published and read, 59

Born to Run (McDougall), 25–26

Boston Marathon bombing, 37

Box, C. J., 63

Breitbart, Andrew, 21–22

Brennan, Jack, 67

Bress, Bill, 135–136

broadcast career, 108

broadcasting, interns in, 54

Brooks, Arthur, 7, 157–160

  The Road to Freedom, 157

Brown, Willie, 23

Buckley, William F., 22

Bullock, Scott, 134
Burns, Martin, 13, 23, 30, 67, 138
Bush, George W., 49–50
Butler, Alban, *Lives of the Saints*, 150

C
caddying, 106
California Arts Council, 106–107
California, green chemistry
regulations, 110–111
Campbell, Matt, 15
Carr, Dabney, 104
Carswell, Harrold, 106–107
Carville, James, 14–15
Casals, Pablo, 61
Catholic education, 124–125
Celestine Prophecy (Redfield), 138
Chapman, Lynne, 68
Chapman University, 113
School of Law, 107–108
Chaput, Charles, 134
charity, anonymous, xxiii
charter school movement, 122
Cheney, Dick, 110
Cheney, Lynne, 67, 110
children
giving and receiving among, xii
impact of family dynamics,
94–95
impact of negative behavior on,
86
impact on perspectives, 82
time with, 83
choice
energy as, 15
good humor as, 44
Christians, perspective for work, 116
A Christmas Carol (Dickens),
117–118
church, 133–147

benefits of attending, 144–147, 155
giving as teaching of, 144
need for, 142–144
Church of Jesus Christ of Latter-day
Saints, 140–141
Churchill, Winston, 17, 118
Clean Water Act, 134
coaches, 17
colleges, and teachers, 123
The Color of Rain (Spehn and Spehn),
65–66
Colson, Charles, 30–31, 112
comedians, as radio guests, 40–41
community
church as, 143
and happiness, 158–159
companionship, 35
congressional elections in 1994, 139
conservatives, conferences of, 158
controversy, avoiding at family
gatherings, 95
Corey, Barry, 113
courage, xi, xvii
coworkers, 105–118
Cox, Chris, 139
Craig, William Lane, 54
cruelty, 86, 155

D
Dailey, Julie, 127
Dalai Lama, xii, 30–31, 41
Dan the Skimmer Target, 20, 25
Dan the Sub Man, 20, 25
Dawkins, Richard, 42
DeCrane, Father, 134
Denver, Rorke, 57–58
Damn Few, 58
Devil at My Heels (Zamperini), 11
Dickens, Charles, *A Christmas Carol*,
86–87, 117–118

disappointments, response to, 61–62
disinterest, 86
Disraeli, Benjamin, 115
doing good, to achieve happiness, 160
Doti, Jim, 113
Douthat, Ross, *Bad Religion*, 124–125
Dreyfuss, Richard, 23, 119–120

E
earned success, 7, 159, 161
Eastman, John, 109
education, 82
    Catholic, 124–125
    public, 82, 125–126
Eisenhower, David, xxiii, xxv, 67
    Eisenhower at War, 85
    Going Home to Glory, 85
Emanuel, Rahm, 83–84
The Embarrassed Believer (Hewitt), 142
empathy, 29–38
    action from, 34
    presence and, 34–35
    and proximity, 32
    vs. sympathy, 33
encouragement, 3–10
    from friends, 102–103
    importance of, 7–8
    self-esteem and, 6–7
    of spouse, 77
Endangered Species Act, 134
energy, 11–18, 144
    as choice, 15
energy transfer, 14
enthusiasm, 19–28, 144
    contagious, 26
entitlement, vs. gratitude, 64
Epperson, Stu, 67
Escalante, Jaime, 121
Essays (Montaigne), 97

eternity, 42
Euripides, 104
evangelization, 27
evil, hierarchy of, 50
exclusivity, 51–52
expectations, 94
extrinsic reward, 129

F
Fahy, Terry, 109
failures, response to, 61–62
faith, 115
    and happiness, 158–159
    opponents of, 152
    as television topic, 30, 138
family
    dynamics of, 94
    as givers, 91–95
    and happiness, 158–159
    vs. work, 139
Feinberg, Michael, 121
Fenty, Joe, 33
Fielding, Fred, 67, 109
First Principles (Hewitt), 58, 98
Fitting, Mrs., 67, 124
Fixx, Jim, *Book of Running*, 26
Fletcher, Danielle Howe, 68
Flynn, Vince, 22–23
Ford, Henry, xxi
forgiveness, 89
Foxworthy, Jeff, 40–41
Franklin, Benjamin, 14, 53
Friday Night Lights (television), 153
friends, as givers, 97–104
friendships, 102
    loss of, 103
Friess, Foster, 113
Friess, Lynne, 113
Fuentes, Tom, xix–xxv, 102

INDEX

G

Gallagher, Mike, 108
The Game of Thrones (Martin), 50
Gaunt, Loie, 67
Gearan, Mark, 100
generosity, xvii, xix–xxvi, 146
Germain, Marc, 109
Getty, Jean Paul, xxi
Gibbons, John, 97–98
gift circle, 73
gifts, those producing happiness, xvi–xvii
giving, as church teaching, 144
God, xvii
    market for books about, 142
God Is Not Great (Hitchens), 54
Going Home to Glory (Eisenhower), 85
Goldberg, Jonah, 158
Gonzales, Saul, 23
good humor, 39–47
    as choice, 44
    limits to giving, 46
    perspective and, 41
good taste, essence of, 52–53
Goodwin, Doris Kearns, *Team of Rivals*, 32
Gottesman, Rick, 65
graciousness, 49–55
    and situational awareness, 52
gratitude, xxiv, 57–69, 144
    vs. entitlement, 64
"Great Books on the Radio" series, xiv
Great Hearts Academies system, 121, 123
greatness, 161
grief, shared experience of, 34
Growing Up Colt (McCoy), 17
Guarnieri, Patti, 99
Guarnieri, Rob, 99–100

H

habits, 66
Hannity, Sean, 84
happiness, xii, xiv–xv, 158
    gifts producing, xvi–xvii
    of Harvard alumni, 163–164
    and material wealth, xxi
    Prager on, 39
    precondition for, xxii
    spouse and, 77
Harris, Sam, 42
Harvard University, 163
Hauser, Dick, 67, 109
Hauth, Russ, 67, 109
Hestenes, Roberta, 30–31
Heston, Charlton, 120
Hewitt, Bill, 137
Hewitt, Grace, 66
Hewitt, Hugh, 66
    The Embarrassed Believer, 142
    First Principles, 98
    In, But Not Of, 142
    Talking with Pagans, 152
Hickson, Janet, 110
Hillenbrand, Laura, *Unbroken*, 11
Hillsdale College, 113
Hitchens, Christopher, 42, 53–54, 145
    God Is Not Great, 54
Hoover, Fred, 67, 124, 127, 128–130
hope, 45
Horner, Connie, 67, 110
hospitality, xxiii
Hruska, Roman, 107
Huffington, Arianna, 84
Hughniverse, 55n
humans, significance of life, 153–154
humility, 126
hypercriticism, 86

I–K

inclusiveness, 50

indifference, 86

ingratitude, 86

Injured Marine Semper Fi Fund, 35–37

"The Inner Ring" (Lewis), 51–52

interns, in broadcasting, 54

interviews, xii–xiii

    of close friends, 102

Janura, Jan, 3, 6

Jefferson, Thomas, 104

Johnson, Samuel, 59

Karrenbauer, Ron, 67, 124, 127

KCET TV, 138

Keating, Thomas, 30–31

kindness, 155

KIPP (Knowledge Is Power Program), 9, 121–122

Knox, John, 42

Kobin, Bill, 30, 139

Konerko, Mary Jean (sister), 124, 126

Kramer, Sidney, 120

Kudlow, Larry, 157, 160n

Kushner, Harold, 30–31, 34

Kushner, Jerry, 102

L

LaRock, Mrs., 67, 124

lassitude, 86

A Last Quartet (movie), 60–61

Laurie, Greg, 112, 138

Lazar, Tex, 67

LeCarré, John, *Tinker, Tailor, Soldier, Spy*, 53

Lemann, Nick, 62

lethargy, 13, 15

Levin, Mark, 84, 121

Lewis, C. S., 94, 126

    "Christianity and Culture," 116

"The Inner Ring," 51–52

Mere Christianity, 13, 137–138

Out of the Silent Planet, 50

Perelandra, 50

That Hideous Strength, 50

"The Weight of Glory," 51, 115–116

Lieberman, Joe, 101

life

    most important things in, xxi

    significance of, 153–154

Life and Times, 13, 30, 67, 138

Lileks, James, 20–21

Lives of the Saints (Butler), 150

Lobdell, Bill, 101–102

    Losing My Religion, 5–6

Long, Rob, 158

Lord of the Rings (Tolkien), 50

Losing My Religion (Lobdell), 5–6

M

MacKinnon, George, 67

Maddox, Kerman, 13, 67, 108

Malone, Jim, 137

Mamet, David, 83

Manchester, William, 17–18

marriage

    problems with, 75–76

    reciprocity of giving in, 77

Marrison, Patt, 67

Martin, George R. R., *The Game of Thrones*, 50

Martinez, Ruebén, 13, 67

Mary Aloysius (sister), 67

Mary Benedicte (sister), 67

Mary Columba (sister), 67, 124

Mary Neal (sister), 67, 124

Mary Timothy (sister), 67

Matalin, Mary, 14–15

material wealth, and happiness, xxi, 164

Mathews, Jay, *Work Hard, Be Nice*, 9, 121

Maxwell, Neal, 30–31, 140–141

McCain, John, 101

McCoy, Brad, *Growing Up Colt*, 17

McDougall, Christopher, *Born to Run*, 25–26

McGuire, Molly, 99

McNulty, Liz, 110

Meacham, Jon, 104

Medved, Michael, 101, 108

Meese, Edwin, 67, 110

men, unhappiest age, 159

Mere Christianity (Lewis), 13, 137–138

Miller, Joel, 27

Minghella, Anthony, 120

ministry, 145–146

Minneapolis Star Tribune, 20–21

modeling energetic behavior, 15

Mokris, Phil, 98

Montaigne, Michel de, *Essays*, 97

Moody, D. L., 151–152

moral choices, 153

Mormons, 140–141

Morrison, Patt, 13, 108

Morrissey, Ed, 76

Morrissey, Marsha, 76

mothers, encouragement for, 8

movies, 60

Mulkerin, Paul, 100

Murray, Cecil, 30–31

N

Naber, John, 12

Nasr, Seyyed Hossein, 30–31

National Endowment for the Humanities, 110

National Review, 21

National Review Institute, 157

New York Times, 124–125

Nicomachean Ethics (Aristotle), xii

Nist, Father, 134

Nixon, Richard, 67, 111

non-confrontation, 140

nonbeliever, benefits of faith community participation, 144–145

Nouwen, Henri
The Return of the Prodigal Son, 88–89
Sabbatical Journey, 88

O–P

O'Brian, Patrick, 162

Ochoa, Anthony, 112n

O'Connor, Larry, 22

Oliva, George, 67, 135–136

Orange County Children and Families Commission, 106

ordinary people, absence of, 51

Out of the Silent Planet (Lewis), 50

The Outpost (Tapper), Tapper, Jake, 33

Pado, Tom, 134

Parental Guidance (movie), 75

parents
as givers, 81–89
happiness of child and, xii

patience, 33
vs. empathy, 31

Patterson, Ben, 137

Patterson, Duane, 12, 67, 68

PBS, *Searching for God in America*, 29–30, 139–140, 141

Pelekoudas, Dan, 65

Perelandra (Lewis), 50

perspective, good humor and, 41

Peterson, Mark, 99

Philip, Snow, 68

Phillips, John, 98

Phillips, Scott, 99
Pisa, Regina, 100
Pisanelli, Steven, 99
political differences, 154
Poneman, Dan, 100
poverty, and happiness, xxii
Prager, Dennis, xiii, 46–47, 101, 108
    on happiness, 39
prayer, 78, 150
priority, 150
Products Liability Advisory Council, 14
professional colleagues, 112
professional self, those helping to develop, 114
proximity, and empathy, 32
public education, 82, 125–126

R
radio show, 135–136, 142
Ramsey, Adam, 68
Reagan, Ronald, xx
reciprocity of giving, in marriage, 77
Redfield, James, *Celestine Prophecy*, 138
Reid, Paul, 17
relationships
    with family, 91–92
    with God, 149
religious belief, good humor and, 42
The Return of the Prodigal Son (Nouwen), 88–89
returned gifts, 74–75
Reynolds, Greg, 99
The Road to Freedom (Brooks), 157
Robb, Roger, 67
Robert, Linda, 11–12
Roberts, John, 58
Roberts, Mark D., 101–102, 137
Rohl, A. T., 66, 162–163

Rohl, Margret, 66
Roman Catholic church
    bishops' letters on nuclear weapons, 137
    sexual scandals, 6, 125
Romney, Mitt, 141, 158
Rose, Charlie, 111
rudeness, 86
running, 25

S
Sabbatical Journey (Nouwen), 88
Saddleback Valley Community Church, 133
Salem Communications, 67, 108
Santore, Mr., 67, 124
Santucci, Kathy, 67, 124
Scully, Vince, intern efforts for interview, 54–55
Searching for God in America (PBS), 29–30, 139–140, 141
security clearances, 107
self-esteem, encouragement and, 6–7
self-importance, 163
serial enthusiasm, 20
Silva, Daniel, 63
situational awareness, and graciousness, 52
Slen, Peter, 62
Smith, William French, 67, 109–110
soldiers, 160–161
South Africa, mission trip, 27–28, 145
South Coast Air Quality Management District, 107
Spehn, Gina Kell, *The Color of Rain*, 65–66
Spehn, Michael, *The Color of Rain*, 65–66
The Spirit of the Liturgy (Benedict XVI), 27

spouse
  encouragement of, 77
  as giver, 73–79
  number one job of, 75
Stand and Deliver, 121
Stanislaw, Jacquie, 99
Steinsaltz, Adin, 138
Stevenson, Robby, 54
Steyn, Mark, 21, 158
Stone, Oliver, 120
Sullivan, Andrew, 64
Sutherland, Donald, 120
sympathy, vs. empathy, 31, 33

T
Talking with Pagans (Hewitt), 152
Tapper, Jake, 112
  The Outpost, 33
Tardie, Jerry, 102
Taussig, Joe, 162
Taussig, Lulie, 162–163
Taylor, John, 67
Teach for America, 121–122
teachers, 119–131
  encouragement from, 9
  gains from career, 127–130
  students giving to, 126
Team of Rivals (Goodwin), 32
Templeton, Jack, xxii, 113
  Thrift and Generosity, xiii
Templeton, Pina, xiii, 113
Thames, Steve, 28
That Hideous Strength (Lewis), 50
This Week with George Stephanopoulos, 83
Thomas Aquinas, *Summa Theological*, 149–150
Thrift and Generosity (Templeton), xiii

time, with children, 83
Timothy (sister), 124
Tinker, Tailor, Soldier, Spy (LeCarré), 53
Tolkien, J. R. R., *Lord of the Rings*, 50
Tradup, Tom, 68
trust in God, 134
24 (television), 153

U–Z
Ulhman, Tracey, 120
Unbroken (Hillenbrand), 11
unhappy people, 146
  response to, 45
Van Dyke, Dick, 40
volunteering, 146
Walken, Christopher, 60–61
Warren, Rick, 112, 133–135
  The Purpose Driven Life, 133
Was, Mrs., 67, 124
"The Weight of Glory" (Lewis), 51, 115–116
White, David Allen, 41, 117
Wild at Heart, 4
Wilson, Mary Pat, 99
Wilson, Peter, 107
Wolensky, Gary, 14, 109
work
  vs. family, 139
  and happiness, 158–159
  responsibility for, 117
Work Hard, Be Nice (Mathews), 9, 121
Yates, Curtis, 65
Young, Hugh, 14–15
Young Life, 5
Zamperini, Louis, 11–13
  Devil at My Heels, 11

ABOUT THE AUTHOR

HUGH HEWITT IS HOST OF THE NATIONALLY SYNDICATED *Hugh Hewitt Show,* heard coast to coast on the Salem Radio Network Monday through Friday from 6:00 to 9:00 p.m. Eastern. Hewitt is a professor of law at Chapman University Law School and a lawyer in private practice, as well as the author of fourteen previous books on faith, politics, and the law. Hewitt writes weekly for the *Washington Examiner* and TownHall.com, and lectures frequently at colleges and universities across the country. He and his wife, "The Fetching Mrs. Hewitt," live in southern California. They have three children.

Hewitt has been a season ticket holder to the Cleveland

Browns since the franchise returned to the shore of Lake Erie in 1999, a triumph of hope over experience. He also hopes the Indians win a World Series in his lifetime—he was born in Warren, Ohio, in 1956 and the Tribe last won it all in 1948—and that the Ohio State Buckeyes and Notre Dame Fighting Irish alternate national championships. Hewitt has no connection but love to either school, his allegiance being an occasion of grace, not works, and, in fact, is a graduate of Harvard College and the University of Michigan Law School. When asked about the latter affiliation, Hewitt responds that he treated the Wolverine State as the Vikings did much of England for centuries: get in, take what is worth having (in his case, the best legal education in the world), and leave.

Hewitt describes himself as a "layer-cake Christian," an "Evangelical Roman Catholic Presbyterian," and a very slow runner. By his count, in a broadcast career on both television and radio, he has conducted more than ten thousand interviews since it began in 1990. You can find transcripts of many of these interviews, along with the original audio, at Hughniverse.com.

HughHewitt.com

Hughniverse.com

twitter.com/hughhewitt

facebook.com/hughhewittshow